Acknowledgements

Phyllis Carter for proofing and editing.

Aisha Buxton for production.

Students and teachers past and present for making every day a learning opportunity.

Warning label

No holds barred fighting includes contact and can be dangerous. Use proper equipment and train safely. Practice with restraint and respect for your partners. Drill for fun, fitness and to improve skills. Do not fight with the intent to do harm.

No Holds Barred Fighting:

Savage Strikes

The Complete Guide to Real World Striking for NHB Competition and Street Defense

Mark Hatmaker

Tracks Publishing
San Diego, California

Photography by
Doug Werner

No Holds Barred Fighting:

Savage Strikes

The Complete Guide to Real World Striking for NHB Competition and Street Defense

Mark Hatmaker

Tracks Publishing
140 Brightwood Avenue
Chula Vista, CA 91910
619-476-7125
tracks@cox.net
www.startupsports.com

Publisher's Cataloging-in-Publication

Hatmaker, Mark.
No holds barred fighting : savage strikes : the complete guide to real world striking for NHB competition and street defense / Mark Hatmaker ; photography by Doug Werner.
p. cm.
Includes index.
LCCN 2004106288
ISBN 1884654207

1. Hand-to-hand fighting–Training. 2. Wrestling. I. Title.

GV1111.H38 2004 796.81
QBI33-2047

I humbly and respectfully dedicate this volume to Paul Maslak for setting me on the path to empiricism regarding combat analysis.

To the master pugilists who knew more than a trick or two, including Jack Dempsey, Harry Greb, Stanley Ketchel, Dan Hodge, Jimmy Wilde, Gene Tunney and Mickey Walker.

To Doug Werner for allowing me to share in print some of what I've learned.

And to my grandfather, George Washington Goins, who hung a homemade heavy bag from the rafters of his barn and told stories of prizefighters "during the day." My respect for him, his amazing strength well into his 60s, and his love of pugilism influenced my admiration for the game as he knew it.

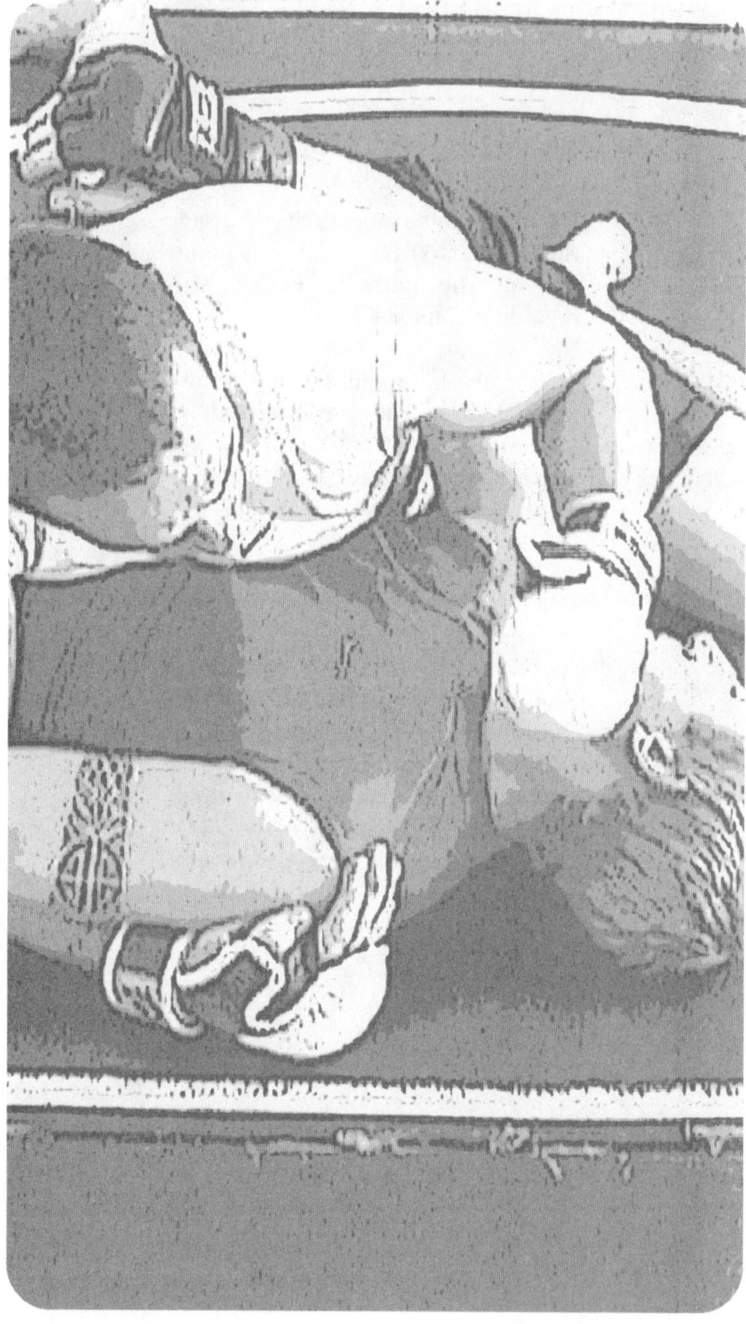

Contents

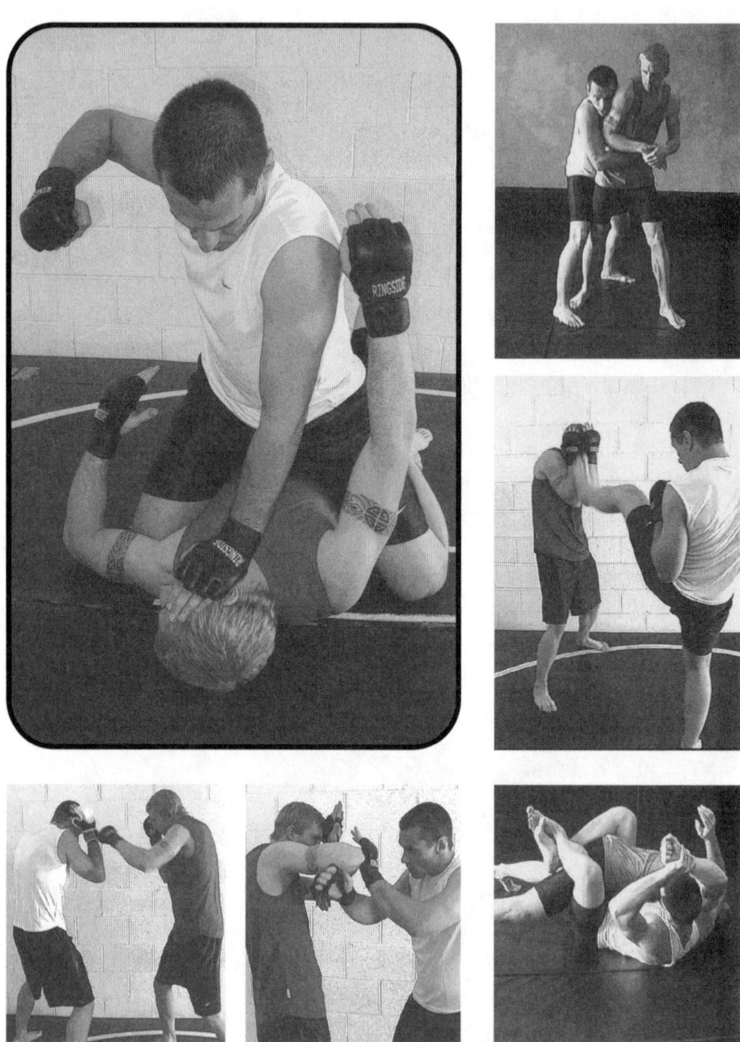

Developing the complete NHB fighter — The NHB athlete has to balance ballistic assaults with concerns about an opponent's incoming strikes and takedown shots and perhaps the subsequent ground game.

Preface

Welcome to the third volume of No Holds Barred (NHB) fighting. The first book was an introduction to the grappling game and provided the fundamentals. The second book built on that base to move you toward constructing intelligent offense and defense chains. This volume provides the nuts and bolts needed to formulate an intelligent, high-percentage striking game taking into consideration the dangers and challenges in this encompassing combat sport. It also explores the arsenal needed to play this game as well as the hows and whys — the strategies, science and drills tied together with the theme of striking not only as a striker but as a grappler.

I'm a strong opponent of mindless cross-training. You shouldn't think you have covered all bases by grappling training on Tuesdays and Thursdays, going to the boxing gym on Wednesdays and Muay Thai class on Saturdays. All that does is expose you to three different sports.

The NHB athlete has to balance ballistic assaults with concerns about your opponent's incoming strikes and takedown shots and perhaps the subsequent ground game. A sport that encompasses that much has to move beyond mere cross-training and toward unity of information and concepts to provide a more streamlined and intelligent base for the NHB athlete.

With that in mind, don't use this guide as a boxing primer or a compendium of Muay Thai techniques. As much as I respect these two effective sports, that pure mix isn't here. (In the Resources section, I recommend some solid stand-alone texts). What you will find is a distillate of Western striking styles applied specifically to the expansive demands of the NHB game. By keeping in mind this specific approach, I sincerely believe that you will move more rapidly toward athletic optimum.

Finally, there are a few sections on theory including one on physics. Please don't ignore this material. I believe it is perhaps even more important than the arsenal section. Without a true understanding of what goes into a punch, you will throw only something that looks like a punch the rest of your life without getting to the heart of the matter.

A lead-in about leads

Right side forward or left side forward? Power side forward or power side back? Orthodox or southpaw? The answers have probably been decided if you are currently involved in a striking sport. Usually leads are taught by a coach or instructor or what you stepped into naturally after years of observing the striking arts. For those who haven't decided, or for those who wonder why everything in this book is demonstrated from a right side forward lead, read on.

John L. Sullivan

The origins of lead choices illuminate what we see today. In the early days of boxing, the left lead forward was the rule because the majority of human beings are right-handed and use the right arm more frequently. The early pugilists were not known for finesse, and the game was more one of power and cutting the opponent with ripping shots. Since the jab was nonexistent (yep, that's right, no jab) the game was posting (stiff-arming) an opponent with a lead hand and letting go with straight rights and roundhouse swings with the rear hand. Rear hand placement allowed fighters to wind up and really put some hurt in their punches.

When the forward-thinking James J. Corbett (Gentleman Jim) took the heavyweight crown from the heavier, old-school John L. Sullivan (The Great John L) primarily by using the new "technology" of the jab, strikers everywhere latched onto this formidable new development. The jab equalized the hands in the sense that both right and left could now be used for causing damage or making distance. The importance and influence of this development is on par with the debut of the UFC and the return of the integral ground game. This equalization of the hands could have been accomplished by either lead forward, but tradition already had run its roots deep, and the power hand to the rear remained in vogue thanks to another development that came along when Corbett shocked the world with his jab. This was the Marquis of Queensbury's dictate that gloves ("mufflers" as they were known then) would be used in prizefights.

Gloves further entrenched the habit of power side to the rear because with the added protection of "pillows" on the hands, competitors had to strike all the harder to deliver damage to their opponents. So, historically, we have two factors contributing to power side to the rear: bare-knuckle fighters competing in a jab-free era and modern boxers striving to gain knockouts through 16 ounces of protective equipment.

Delivering damage with both hands.

Flash forward to today. Grappling gloves weigh only four to six ounces, so there is little need to get the added boost of power from a rear side placement. And advancements in the "sweet science" have taught today's fighters that brawn isn't necessarily the key to knockout power, but rather timing and directed mass. Modern fighters have added a host of uses to lead and rear hands and knockouts statistically are just as likely to occur from either hand.

Let's move the lead bias from the boxer/kickboxer perspective to the NHB athlete. The NHB competitor has more concerns to deal with than the pure striker. He has to strike and defend strikes, manage his own takedown shots and shoot defenses from whatever lead he chooses.

I highly recommend coordinated side forward, not power side to the rear or power side forward. By placing the hand you sign your name with to the fore, you will be placing in the lead the hand that has the best coordination, timing, control of precise motor skills and speed. The fact that you have placed your stronger hand (as dominant hands invariably are) in the lead improves your chances of making each jab heavier and each lead hook and uppercut a more likely KO weapon. By placing the subdominant hand to the rear, you take the "weaker" of the two hands and give it extra power by adding distance and arc to each shot. Rather than put all eggs into the power-shot basket, power has been equalized and speed and precision increased by utilizing a coordinated lead forward.

To summarize:
1. NHB requires that you evade shots — a coordinated side forward will ensure optimum reaction time for defense.

2. NHB requires precision on shots — coordinated side forward ensures you have your "best foot forward" for these gambits.

3. NHB requires strong striking and does not have the onus of "over-padded" gloves to prevent each punch from meaning something — coordinated side forward bestows both hands with formidable speed and striking power.

These arguments notwithstanding, if you are already comfortable as a power side to the rear fighter, then chances are you may not want to spend 30 days or more to retrain your neural network. The lead preference is only a recommendation and not a prerequisite to make full use of the material that follows. I started out as an orthodox striker and made the transition seven years into my training, and I never looked back.

I advocate running every drill through both leads. NHB has such dynamically changing positions, both on your feet and on the mat, that sometimes lead preference can become a moot point. When running every drill through both leads, you will recognize a lead preference since you will be more fluid on one side. But you will be thankful that you have run both sides through their paces in the inevitable eventuality that you get "turned" in your footwork and must (even momentarily) work from a less familiar side.

Isaac Newton and Jack Dempsey

Quite a pair, huh? The scientific giant who formulated calculus and the Manassa Mauler. What could they possibly have in common? It is my contention that Newton's Second Law of Motion was embodied quite ably (and viciously, I might add) in every punch thrown by Dempsey — not that he was aware of Newton or his laws.

Sir Isaac Newton

Jack Dempsey

This short physics lesson is the key to help unlock the secrets to KO power. Most folks judge power by the breadth of an athlete's shoulders. Some, by the windup in a Toughman competitor's Sunday punch.

Power is actually found in the following equation:

F = ma or Force = mass x acceleration

Let's look at the equation in the fighting context:

KO Power = Directed Body Mass x Strike Speed

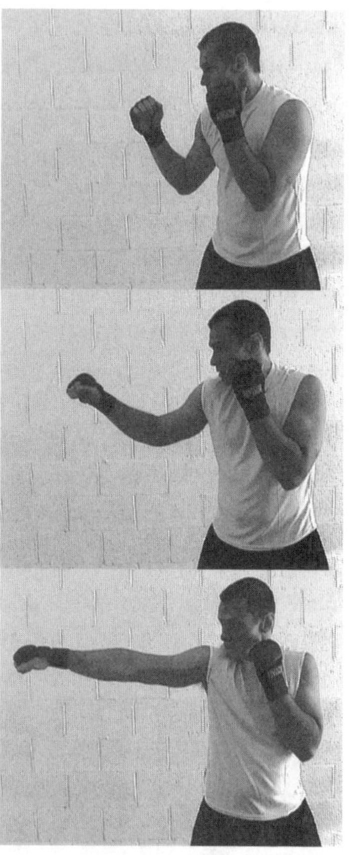

An arm punch has no weight behind it.

Knockouts (or simply the increase in punching power) can be accomplished by learning the core principles of moving body mass in the direction of your strikes along an efficient plane or arc and whipping or snapping punches to ensure speed. In fact, the usual practice of attempting to "put some muscle" into your shots can be an impediment to KO goals. Using the primary striking tool, the jab, illustrates the importance of Newton's Second Law of Motion.

First, stand before a heavy bag or have a partner face you with a focus mitt. Using only arm and shoulder musculature, blast the pad with one good shot without taking a step forward. Just set, wind up and hit. Next, strive to hit the pad as fast as you can. Don't wind up or attempt to put any muscle into the shot. Just feel the need for speed and let loose. These two methods and all points in between are usually what striking novices do (this includes someone with years of experience who hasn't bothered to absorb his physics lessons).

The first striker in the above example is all about windup and what can be accomplished with brawn. These muscle strikes can hit with some impact, but intention is telegraphed by the windup and are noticeably slower because of the need to wind up (even incremental windups are unnecessary). Because of the reliance on muscular force, they devolve quickly when fatigue and other causes of physical entropy occur in a combat sport. The latter technical approach, the speed demon, can also score a hit, but with little consequence for having done so. NHB is not a game of glorified tag found in the current incarnations of most traditional martial arts. Speed shots (or show jabs) may find their marks but will do little if anything to stop an opponent.

If these two approaches are filtered through Newton's Second Law, we learn why they are inefficient and ineffective. In the muscle-only punch, we are ignoring the two components that produce force. By emphasizing power over speed, there is negligible acceleration to factor in. By choosing to use only upper-body muscle mass to launch the jab, we have ignored two thirds of our body mass that could have been involved in the punch. In the speed-only jab, pains have been taken to raise the acceleration bar but the only mass factored in is that of the jab limb itself, which is of nominal effect when compared to the entire body mass.

So, how do you increase strike mass while focusing on speed? Simply do what all great wrestlers and boxers

This punch is powered by COM. Note the hip thrust.

do. Use center of mass (COM) in each and every technique. COM, as it applies to wrestling and grappling, already has been addressed in our first two guides, *No Holds Barred Fighting* and *More No Holds Barred Fighting*.

COM is located in your hips. This is the point or nexus of the body's greatest weight. If you learn to control COM at all times, and to consciously use it in all strikes, you will go a long way toward upping the mass side of the force equation.

To use COM in every strike, it is a good idea to determine how to move COM toward an opponent with the execution of each technique. We will break down the jab to illustrate the concept. The most obvious way to get COM into a jab is to step forward as you punch. But how you step is just as important as the fact that you are stepping. Step directly at an opponent while snapping the leading hip toward him. Since the jab is a lead-hand shot, we shoot the lead side of the pelvis forward. We reverse this for rear-hand shots. I strongly suggest taking a few practice rounds emphasizing direct stepping and COM snapping sans punch. In other words, perform only the step and hip snap without the punch until you feel the coordination of foot placement and hip movement. Once this feels fluid, add the jab into the mix.

The above exercise has shown how to exploit your COM. Now let's look at the acceleration portion of the force equation. Boxing coaches everywhere exhort their fighters to snap their punches. This means to treat the arm like a whip. The fist is the tip of the whip being cracked at the end of the strike, as opposed to just pushing punches. If you snap punches with the whip analogy in mind, speed will increase. Snapping punches also calls for less muscular energy allowing you to conserve stores (always a blessing in the grueling fight game). Once you combine snapping punches (acceleration) with aid of COM (exploiting your mass), you will have maximized the force equation with Newton's Second Law of Motion and Dempsey's philosophy of "bad intentions."

Snap and pop!

Keep these concepts in mind as you approach each component of the arsenal and their subsequent applications in combination work and counter-striking sequences. By breaking down every shot in Newton's calculating fashion and then re-assembling them in the ring, cage or octagon, you will be tuned into the same principle of physics that Dempsey used to rule the world.

A little time for timing

Timing is the ephemeral, but oh so necessary art and science of launching the most effective attack at the specific moment of an opponent's vulnerability. When you see a one-punch knockout or perfectly executed takedown that seems so precise it feels choreographed, you have witnessed good timing. Good timing is Roy Jones, Jr. in the ring or Kevin Jackson pursuing a take-down or Kazushi Sakuraba playing cagey and then executing a double-wrist lock just as Renzo Gracie attempts to pull out of the hold.

Speed of recognition is more important in timing than speed of execution. Don't get me wrong, speed of execution is fantastic, but without choosing the right attack at the right time, most speed is for naught. Sort of an "all flash and no cash" scenario. If we accept the idea that the important aspect of timing is speed of recognition, it is feasible to accept the fact that a honed sense of recognition can trump mere speed of execution. Furthermore, it is more likely for seasoned combat athletes to experience good timing as timing is inculcated by years of training. The more time one puts into efficient (intelligent) training, the better the timing is going to be. In this attribute of timing, at least, age may not necessarily be a factor.

How one trains to better one's timing is just as important as what one trains. I believe timing is taught by repetition, repetition, repetition. The more you perform drills, techniques or concepts in circumstances that mimic the combat environment, the greater the chances that "spontaneous" good timing will emerge. This is akin to the jazz musician drilling scales, modes and chord juxtapositions for his impromptu solos and riffs in jam sessions. Much work precedes perfomances for them to appear effortless. The only tricks are to have mastered the discipline of repetition and to never veer from its wisdom. Then you can allow the training to take over in combat with no thought given to tricks.

An opponent's gift for physical speed of execution can be stymied by pressing the attack and using good timing. An opponent who is pressured has less of an opportunity to mount a thoughtful defense against your steady onslaught. Physical speed is conquered by pressure. Speed without mass behind it can generate no force or stopping power, so by continually pressing the attack, you are able to take the forward momentum of your opponent's mass from the force/stopping power equation leaving him with only speed and less dangerous.

Against a larger opponent, the concept of repetition drilling is ideal so that proper choices at inculcated reference points emerge of their own volition. Timing is crucial against a superior fighter who is labeled tough with a capital "T." One must, of course, prepare beforehand and decide that there are plenty of tough fighters out there, but no one tougher than you in your chosen combat science with your given attributes. Do not be deterred by this psychological snag regarding toughness. Tough is a mind-set.

Superior strength can be thwarted by having had the discipline to drill dogmatically. You should always drill for fighting someone larger, stronger, and tougher. Training to beat inferiors is training to be a bully and not a student of self-defense. The entire aim of training should be to defend or defeat opponents with superior skills or attributes. If this is not the goal in mind, then your training goals and skills will plateau.

Remember, timing comes from repetition. You should train with total mindfulness of this and not mindlessly. Don't hit repetition after repetition by rote, but see, feel, be a part of each and every repetition in your training so that when the time comes for your arsenal to emerge, it can of its own accord. The word training calls to mind a train on its tracks working toward a destination. This metaphor is apt since training, if properly attended to, will naturally follow the rails to victory with little steering needed.

The biggest obstacle to timing is choice. Thinking about what you should or should not do while competing or fighting places too many speed bumps in the process. Think only while training so that it's second nature in the competitive environment. Keep in mind, your good timing can come up against an opponent's good timing — that's when the dance of physical chess happens. This is what we all train for — to hit or submit and not be hit or submitted. You place yourself before opponents who have the exact same goal so it is inevitable that two athletes with good timing will meet and a slippery war ensues. It is for these most challenging and rewarding occasions that you need to train mindfully.

To summarize our good timing training: train mindfully, train repetitively, give it all up and have a good time.

School of hard knocks

Getting hit sucks. It's no fun. Nobody likes to get hit. So why do so many of us choose a sport that is all about getting hit? Because there's nothing quite like a good match to make you feel alive. It's just you and him and nothing else exists. If the mind wanders for a moment — BAM! "Fight Club" had it right (both the novel and the film) — when it's on, it's on and that's all there is. Just you, your opponent and the process of what's happening right now. And really, there aren't too many activities that allow us to experience that in-the-moment flow.

OK, we understand the visceral attraction to the game we play, but that doesn't mean any of us actually likes getting hit. We know it's an inevitability but wonder if there is anything we can do to take those lumps a little easier. Well, not much. It's all in the mind-set. If you love the sport enough — and here I'm talking the whole process — training, drilling, competing — you are already rewarded over and above the occasional beating.

On the other hand, there's the tempered approach, which is actually the wisest. In the tempered approach, one always takes care to train and drill safely. That means proper safety gear (mouthpiece, groin cup, head-gear, sparring gloves), proper ground rules and good refereeing. It also means having a goal in mind before each and every sparring session and match. If you begin a session with a goal in mind, like working the body more or emphasizing footwork, you will direct your attention to the accomplishment of that goal and divert much of it away from the anxiety that can accompany the taking of a few shots.

Keep in mind, no one says you have to take full-bore shots. A fighter can train the striking game his whole life keeping it in the drill-only arena by gearing up and playing a limited contact game. This is optimum for the sports enthusiast who loves the game but isn't looking to pay any bills with it. This limited contact game is akin to the tap protocol in submission wrestling where there is no need to snap a limb to gain a concession. You need only execute good technique. It is quite easy to play a striking game with the same mind-set. Just play with limited or reduced contact and respect the potential damage that a delivered blow can incur.

How to take a punch

Beyond the redirection of attention and the gradual acclimation to harder and harder contact, there is no magic formula or technique to make absorbing impact any easier. It is wise (in addition to the above advice) to become a defensive master. Work each and every defensive movement in drills and call-and-response chains just as assiduously as you train your offense, and you will become a slippery opponent that is not hit often.

Please note that not being hit at all is an impossibility. Recall the words of the great Sugar Ray Leonard, "Fighters get hit; good fighters don't get hit as much." And that's from one of the slickest of the defense artists. If he got hit in his career, you can expect the same. So with Leonard's quote in mind, follow these recommendations:

1. Set your mind straight before sparing. Getting hit is an inevitability.
2. Train your defense as mindfully as you do offense.
3. Drill call-and-response chains diligently — there's no better tool for sparring preparation.
4. Wear proper safety equipment.
5. Work up the contact scale in gradual increments.
6. Never move up the contact scale until ready.
7. Train with good ground rules and supervision.
8. Have a goal in mind before you spar.
9. Never spar angry and never spar an angry opponent. (In other words, check egos at the door.)
10. Last, but not least, have fun.

Bias and the 80/20 rule

I'm going to come clean — I emphasize boxing in NHB striking over kickboxing. That will come as no surprise to those who have thumbed through the book and paid attention to the photos, which show a preponderance of upper-body strikes with a modicum of lower-body shots.

There are two reasons for this bias:

1. Western boxing is one of my great loves and I reflect that in what I advocate for the NHB player.

2. Statistical evidence and the 80/20 rule bear out the wisdom of adhering to boxing as a primary striking base.

The 80/20 principle was first formally observed in 1897 by Italian economist Vilfredo Pareto (the 80/20 principle is sometimes known as The Pareto Principle). The Pareto Principle can be stated in several ways, among them that in business 80% of results come from 20% of efforts. And that 20% of a business's employees are responsible for 80% of the work (an easily observable fact in your own place of employment, I'm sure). Perhaps this is best expressed by Richard Koch who said that a minority of causes, input or effort most always lead to a majority (80%) of the results, output or rewards. Determining what efforts lead to the greatest rewards allows you to prune the low return work and emphasize the high returns.

This rule, as it applies to NHB athletes, states that 20% of a fighter's arsenal or strategies will reap 80% of the victorious results, whereas 80% of an arsenal will return only 20%. Since there are only a few hours in the day allotted for training, it is wise to choose the 20% of your arsenal that accounts for the highest percentage of results. You will be using your time to hone the most valuable techniques to full advantage. Keep in mind that by choosing to emphasize the 20% does not mean that any tool in the arsenal deemed a poor return has to be culled. Try using the 80/20 principle with training time as well. Train your 80% return arsenal for 80% of training time and your 20% return arsenal only 20%.

With the 80/20 principle in mind, how do you decide what portions of your arsenal will provide the highest returns? Observation and the empirical method with a dab of statistics. Case in point: Why is the jab the most utilized weapon in boxing? It's not necessarily the tool with the greatest stopping power and yet it is the most fired punch in the history of the game. The answer lies in its effectiveness. The jab is a fantastic tool for range finding, keeping an opponent off balance, creating cumulative damage, and picking away at an opponent's composure.

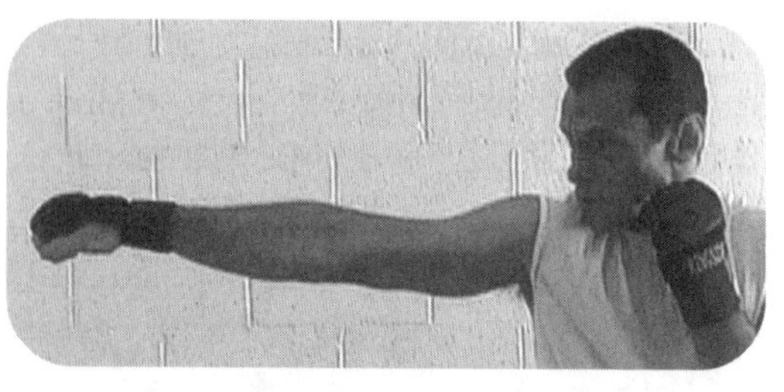

The jab did not arrive upon the scene in its present incarnation until well after the turn of the century. The young sport of English boxing emphasized swinging and roundhouse blows over straight shots. It was only after painstaking development of the jab that its usefulness was recognized and turned into the weapon that should be learned first and used foremost. The methods used to determine the jab's effectiveness were trial, error and observation.

We can turn to the statistical method (so ably pioneered in the combat game by Paul Maslak in the '70s) by observing matches in our chosen sport and tabulating successful striking tools. If one examines the most effective and useful tools in boxing, kickboxing (including Muay Thai and Savate) and NHB, and transfers that data to paper, you get a good look at which efforts fall into the 80/20 rule.

While performing this research, be careful not to give too much weight to the choices between unevenly matched opponents. Because sometimes a very skilled practitioner plays down his level of competition and utilizes strategies and tools he might not normally consider against a better opponent. (Think Roy Jones, Jr. or Sugar Ray Leonard using the bolo punch to play with lesser opponents and not daring to attempt such tactics against true contenders. Or Mike Vanarsdale launching a kicking attack in his UFC debut because he saw it on TV the night before. You can only play such games with opponents not your equal.) To get truly useful information, it is best to pay close attention to matches between competitors on a relatively similar skill level. Then you can better observe what does and does not work in tough conditions and scenarios.

Once the information is tabulated, you will find that hand strikes account for most of the damage, setups, and/or knockouts. (Keep in mind these hand strikes are of the common variety. Very few spinning hand strikes account for significant results in even matches.) Following hands in effectiveness are elbows, knees, head butts and low-line kicks. Although many spectacular knockouts do occur with high-line body and head kicks, they are last in the hierarchy.

Let's take a look at what may be an uncomfortable fact for many striking practitioners who are fans of the kicking game. Although kicking, particularly the Muay Thai variety, is indeed a devastating mode of attack — its effectiveness is beautifully observed in straight Muay Thai or kickboxing matches — it poses less of a threat in NHB or All-In matches. NHB calls for a wide variety of attack opportunities and the ability and willingness of an opponent to execute a fast takedown shot can upset a strategy of primarily kicking. Kicking calls for greater transfers of body mass, therefore combination kicking is a slower attacking strategy than combination punching.

Punching does not require extreme body mass transfers. Though there are many phenomenally fast and talented kicking athletes on the NHB scene, statistical information states that kicking should be only 20% of training time for the average NHB athlete who wants to invest his efforts in maximum return activities.

Speed, precision, high-number combinations, and protection of your base (balance) against an opponent's takedown attempts are best executed and maintained by adhering to the upper-body tools as primary weapons. You should bring the elbows, knees and head butts into play only in clinch situations. A fighter should use low-line kicks as spice or test-probes in a long-distance game in which his shot is not likely to be disrupted.

Even in the majority of kickboxing matches, the hands are primary finishers or what initiated the damage, then the kicking attacks follow. Many kickboxing commissions recognize this fact and apply kick minimums to keep the game from devolving into a straight boxing match. In some Savate matches, more than two punches in succession are prohibited. Muay Thai enthusiasts, who wish to supplement the low-line attacks found in this book, should see the resources section for a few excellent texts on the subject.

1 Stance, footwork, upper body mobility and rolling a fist

NHB striking stance

Good base is fundamental. Whether on your feet or on the mat, a fighter must be firmly in control of his balance. And it's important to control your opponent's balance as well. Before hitting, make sure you can stand. You can generate solid strikes only from a solid stance.

Things to keep in mind about good standing base:

1. An often quoted statistic is that 90% of fights end up in a clinch and on the ground.

2. Keep in mind that almost 100% of fights begin standing up.

3. In competition the fighter who scores the take down ends up the winner 90% of the time.

A fighter needs to play the odds and make sure that he is strong on his feet to reduce the chance of being struck or taken down and to increase the odds of striking or scoring the takedown.

The stance is not static, although we will describe it in a static position. Once you are able to emulate the stance, start moving around with it. Be fluid while maintaining the integrity of the stance principles. The following chapter on movement will go a long way toward helping you move intelligently.

Assuming the NHB striking stance

We will assume a right lead. Pretend that you are standing on a clock facing noon. Step the right foot to 2 o'clock and your left foot to 8 o'clock. Keep the upper body facing noon. The weight is distributed equally between your feet with soles in contact with the floor, but feel the weight more through the balls of the feet. Knees are bent carrying the body midway between an upright position and a crouch.

Looking at the stance head-on, see that the hands are up, fists clenched loosely with the rear-hand touching the cheek and the lead fist positioned at shoulder level approximately 12 inches in front of the lead shoulder. The rear arm rests on the ribs, while the lead forearm assumes an exact parallel position approximately six inches in front of the lead-side rib cage. The chin is tucked toward the breastbone while lifting the lead shoulder to protect the jaw. This mimics a hands-free telephone position in which you would hold a handset between your chin and shoulder. This hand and arm position is good cover for defending strikes.

Correct NHB stance

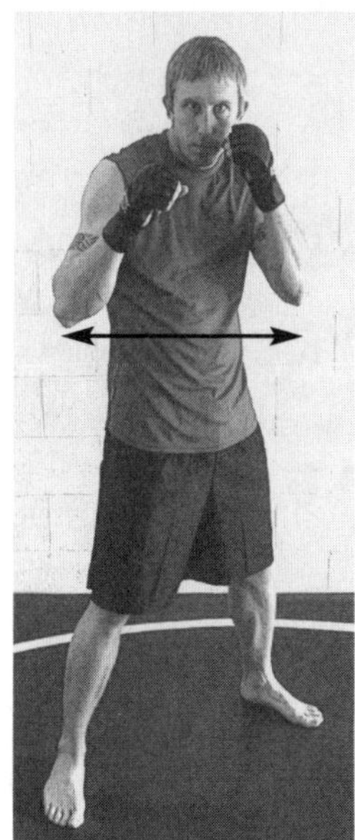

Flared elbows — a common mistake.

Resist the temptation to flare the elbows at the bottom of this defensive shell creating an inverted **V**. Doing so allows an opponent easy access to land body shots.

This is a modified boxing stance. A fighter must guard against strikes as well as take-down efforts. The stance is a bit wider and lower than a boxer's stance to make a stronger base. With the shooting aspect in mind, avoid a completely upright and narrow-based boxer's stance by keeping the 2 o'clock and 8 o'clock foot position wider than usually observed in straight boxing. Use a mirror to check position. Fall into the stance naturally and make sure that all elements are present so that you will be working from maximum offensive and defensive advantage. Once you feel comfortable falling into position naturally, turn the page and we'll get moving.

Step and drag allows a fighter to move while maintaining maximum stability.

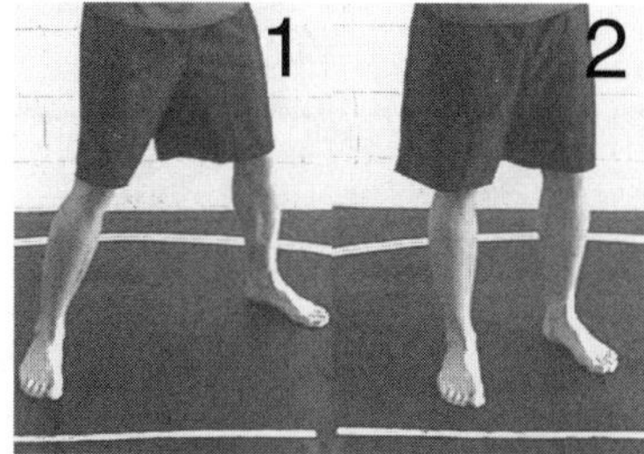

Common footwork errors include stepping feet too close together and crossing legs (below).

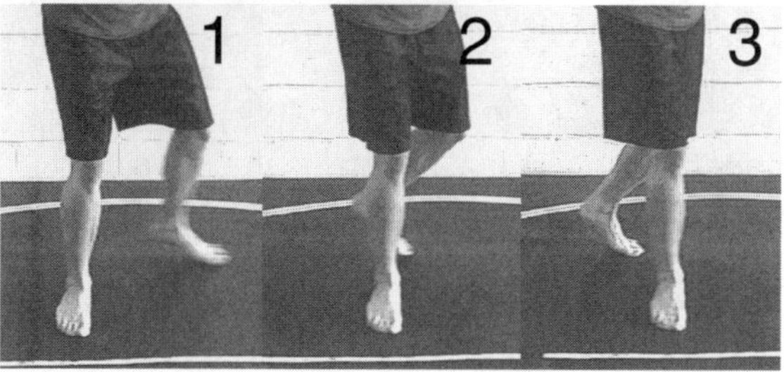

Footwork

Now, let's learn to move within that stance. Here are some basics pertinent to all movement on the feet. Always keep feet in contact with the mat. No hopping, skipping or Ali shuffle footwork is recommended for NHB movement.

Step and drag

In all stepping motions, use a step and drag that allows you to keep at least one foot in contact with the mat at all times.

Step and drag in the direction you intend traveling by moving the foot closest to that direction first. In other words, if you want to step forward, step the forward foot first and drag the rear foot behind it. To go back, step with the rear foot first and drag the lead foot. To go right, move the right foot first and drag the left. To go left, move the left foot first and drag the right.

Pivoting — Another basic move that maintains the structural integrity of the fighting stance. Here around the right foot.

There are eight directions to step. Imagine you are standing on a clock face. Work the step and drag in each direction to refine the movement. Don't cross your feet or place them closer together than shoulder width, otherwise base is compromised and you become an easy target.

Pivot

A pivot is a defensive step executed by putting all weight on the ball of your lead foot and swinging the other foot 90 degrees right or left. The pivot is used to deflect a rushing opponent. Work the pivot assiduously in both directions.

Shift step

The shift step is another useful offensive and defensive footwork pattern. The shift step calls for a change in your stance lead. It is used while retreating or advancing. To perform, step your lead foot to the rear and assume the formerly rear hand as the lead guard. You can also shift step forward by stepping the rear side forward into a new lead. Work several rounds with

Shift step — Switching leads with steps back (top) and forward.

the shift step making sure to fall into proper stance each time. Combine the shift step and the pivot — shift step back from a rush and then pivot to cut yourself out of an opponent's line of attack.

Maintain the structural integrity of the stance while using the above permutations. It is very common to lose the upper-body position when moving in the beginning. You are so busy concentrating on your feet that the upper body goes to hell. Work this movement in front of a mirror so that you can catch any errors and make corrections.

I suggest six rounds of footwork in the mirror and then another six rounds with a partner. Have a partner dictate direction and pace while you follow his movement for a round and then switch roles. Be diligent about adhering to precise technique and attempt to stump one another with variations.

Movement on the feet is one of the least developed attributes for NHB fights. Train it well to move higher in your game. Next we look at a few upper-body maneuvers to add to the defensive arsenal.

Upper body mobility

Mobility acquired by intelligent footwork is extremely important. Footwork is how a fighter maneuvers himself into offensive and defensive ranges. But the subject

Pull — Proper form (above and immediate right).

Take care not to lose guard when pulling back (far right).

of mobility, with the steps learned in the previous chapter, is not complete without adding the following upper-body evasions.

Pull

The pull is merely leaning the upper body away from an incoming strike. The pull does not need an extreme angle. That calls for loading too much weight onto the rear foot, leaving the lead leg essentially weightless and susceptible to an easy takedown shot.

Be careful not to execute lazy pulls in which you pull from an opponent's strike but return too slowly. Pulls are meant to be executed in rapid style in both the positive and the negative portions of the movement. Snap the torso back in a ballistic manner and return it to its previous upright posture just as quickly, prefer-

To slip left, bend the knees and turn your upper body so that the right shoulder points toward your left knee. To slip right, bend knees and point left shoulder toward right knee.

ably while returning an offensive salvo of your own.

Slip

A slip could be defined as a lateral pull to either the left or right. This is correct in a broad sense, but a simple lateral motion with the torso upsets the base too much to be of value for the NHB athlete. There is a more efficient manner in which to laterally evade incoming blows and that allows you to stay properly weighted while bringing you closer to an opponent in order to launch counters at open targets.

The true slip is accomplished by bending at the knees and remembering the opposite shoulder/opposite knee rule: To slip left, bend the knees and turn your upper body so that the right shoulder points toward your left knee. To slip right, bend knees and point left shoulder toward right knee.

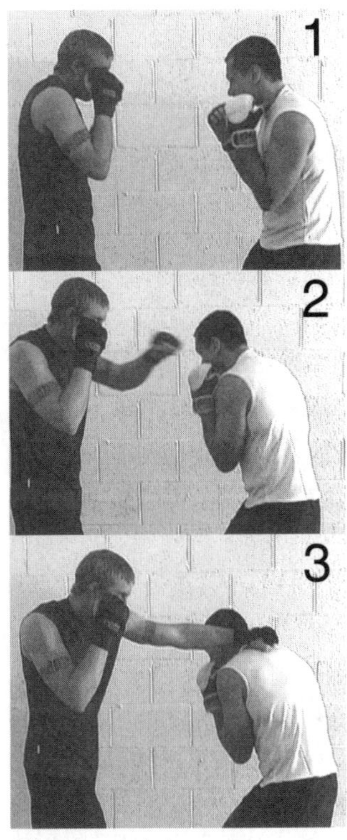

Slipping a jab.

It is important to realize that you will be bending only a little at the waist. The body's descent is accomplished by bending the knees and pointing the shoulder to the opposite knee. It is acceptable in boxing to execute extreme bends at the waist because the boxer has only the uppercut to fear in this position. In NHB we must fear the knee, descending strikes to the back of the head, neck and upper back, and of course, the snap-down.

Bob and weave

Because of the above considerations, I do not advocate the upper-body maneuver commonly known as the bob and weave. Although effective in straight boxing matches, it poses too many offensive opportunities for an opponent. It is not recommended.

Duck

This final upper-body maneuver is accomplished almost solely by the legs. Bend at the knees, not the waist. Bending at the waist puts you in the same danger from attacks as bobbing and weaving.

There is a precise technique to use that will place you in range for follow-up offense. Imagine that there is a

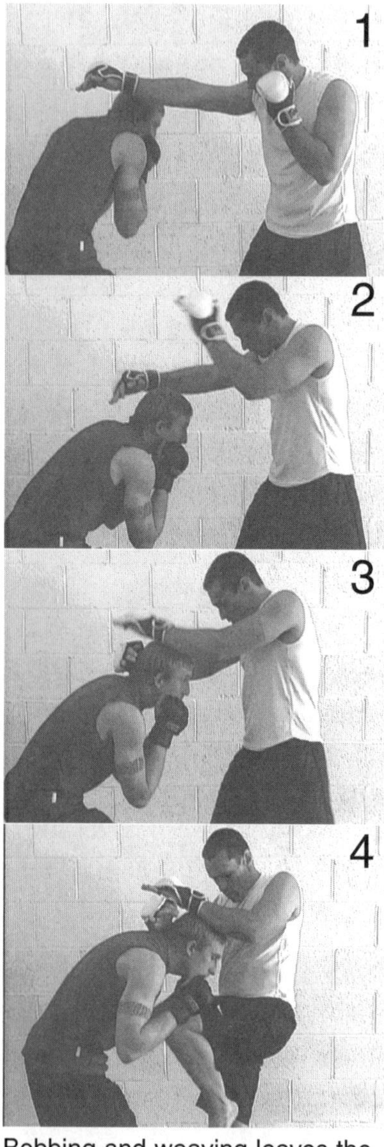

Bobbing and weaving leaves the NHB fighter open to easy offensive assaults.

large capital letter **V** between you and your opponent. The top stroke of each end of the **V** ends at each of your jaw lines. To execute a proper duck, step forward with the lead foot and bend at the knees to descend at a downward angle along your half of the **V**. At the bottom of the motion, as the attacker's strike bites air, stand up into your opponent. Come up at an angle along his side of the **V**. This maneuver puts you almost directly on top of an opponent.

Drill each of these movements in isolation for several rounds and then in tandem with each footwork pattern for several more rounds. Think of footwork and maneuverability analogous to armed transport. Striking weapons are your armory but without the delivery

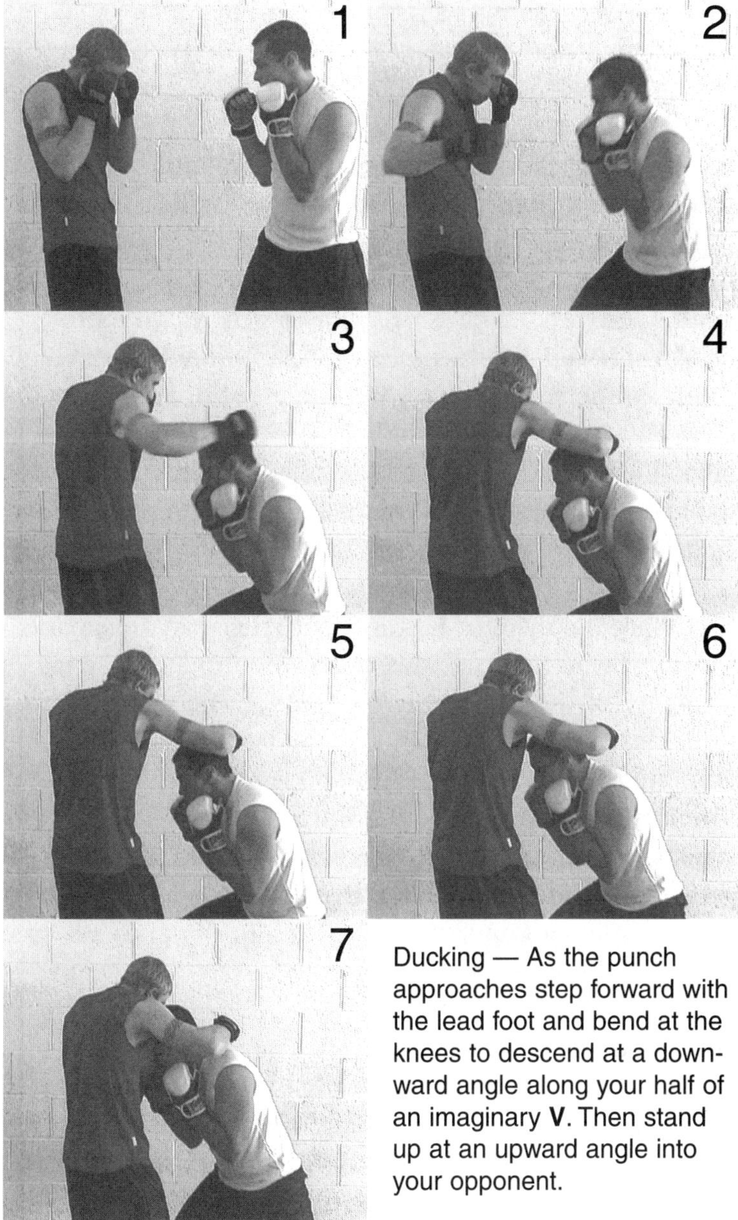

Ducking — As the punch approaches step forward with the lead foot and bend at the knees to descend at a downward angle along your half of an imaginary **V**. Then stand up at an upward angle into your opponent.

and evasion systems of footwork and upper-body maneuvers, you may have little opportunity to launch them.

With maneuvering concepts in place, it's time to consider the complete NHB arsenal.

Fist rolling

Yeah, I know ... making a fist. Basic stuff. Been there, done that. Well, let's make sure we know what we're doing. Modern 16-ounce gloves and hand wraps have changed the science of making a fist. NHB gloves are close in size and weight to the "mufflers" from the early days of the gloved era when fist-rolling was practiced as it was in the bare-knuckle days.

If you are involved in Eastern martial arts in any shape, form or fashion you've heard "strike with the first two knuckles of the fist" (index and middle finger knuckles). This supposedly has the twofold benefit of aligning the bones of your fist perfectly with the forearm bones that allows a more structurally sound striking weapon. Utter BS. The second myth bandied about is the idea that one can sight between these two knuckles like a gun sight to better aim punches. BS cubed and served cold.

Here's how the old-timers did it when they were punching hard through more than 70 rounds. Roll the fist by closing from the outside fingers in (little finger followed by the ring finger, middle finger and then the index finger.) Fold the thumb over the middle joints of the index and middle fingers. You have now fist-rolled into a solid block. Look at the striking surface. Strike

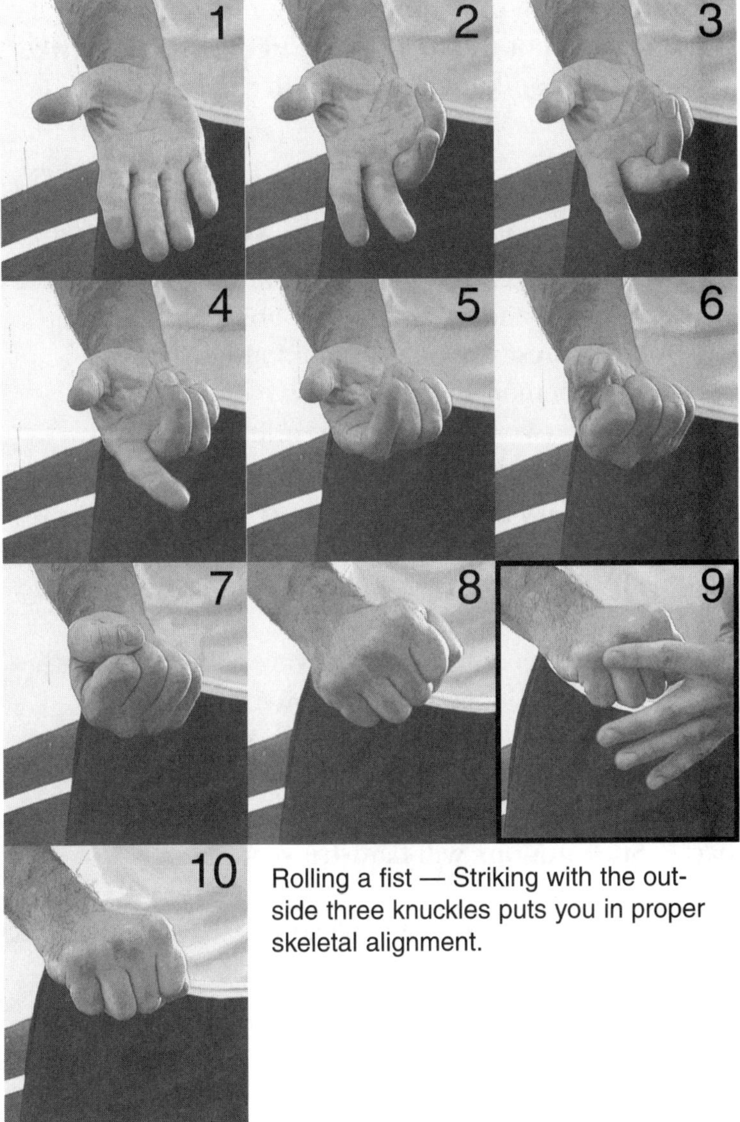

Rolling a fist — Striking with the outside three knuckles puts you in proper skeletal alignment.

with the outside three knuckles (the middle, ring and little fingers), not the first two. Moreover, do not strike with just the top knuckles but with the entire three-finger area.

Striking with the outside three knuckles puts you in proper skeletal alignment. All strikes will line up naturally with the forearm's radius and ulna bones and will prevent rolling and spraining the wrist. The Eastern method is a prescription for sprained wrists from repeated punching against hard, live opponents. Compare the two alignments by rolling a fist and placing each version against a wall. Then push through with all your weight. This simple experiment shows instantly which version provides more stability. Feel the wobble in the Eastern method? You do not want that.

Gun-sighting has nothing to do with how the body works. You don't need to sight down the hands to reach forward and pick up a pencil. Kinesthetic perception takes care of that. Precision punching is gained through drilling, not sighting down an imaginary barrel. Such notions will hamstring progress.

That's it. Now that you can roll a proper fist, let's throw some leather.

NHB arsenal

Here are the weapons shown with proper execution. I suggest working each in isolation rounds before using them in combinations (see Combinations).

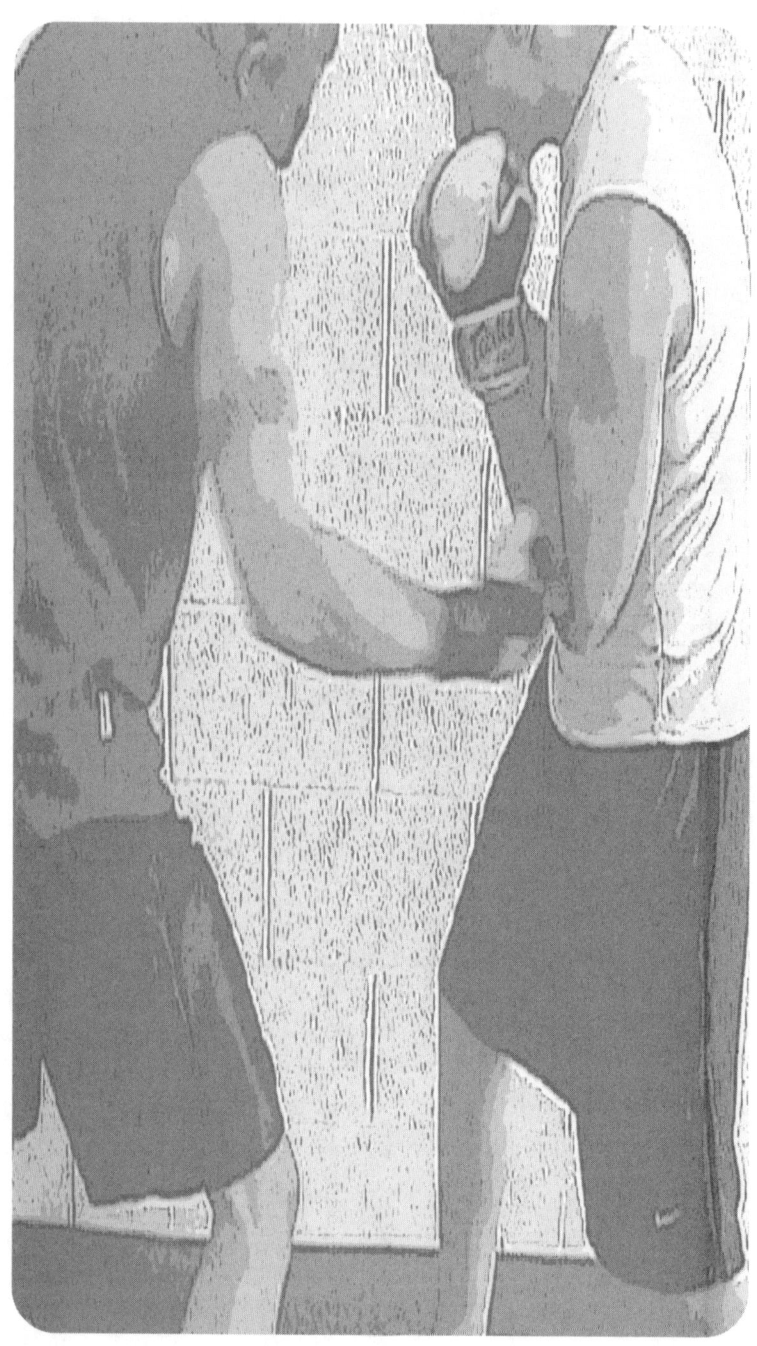

2 Straight boxing arsenal

Jab

- The king of weapons is addressed first.
- Step forward while firing the punch directly from your lead-ready position.
- Rotate the fist to palm down position upon impact.
- Time the impact to coincide with the exact moment your lead foot plants with the step you take for maximum power.

- At the end of the jab, your lead shoulder will be hunched high to protect your lead jaw line from incoming attacks.
- Return the jab along the same path — no deviation.

Cross / rear straight

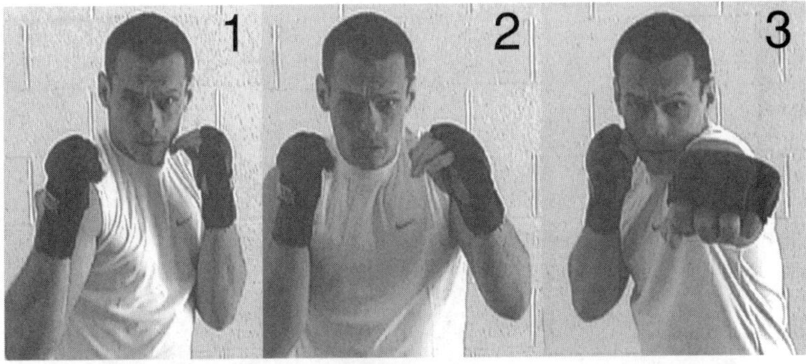

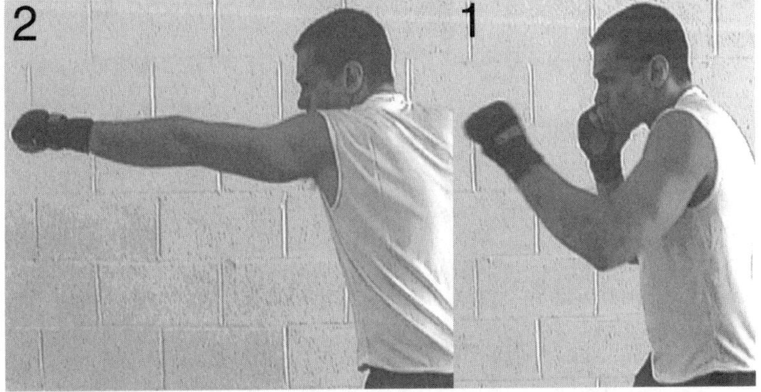

- This is primarily a follow-up strike that is seldom used as a lead. Many fighters consider this their Sunday punch.
- To execute, take a step forward with the lead foot while turning your torso so the rear shoulder points at the target.
- Fire the punch straight from its guard position rotating the fist palm down upon impact.
- Time the step and punch impact as in the previous technique.
- At the end of the punch, your lead fist pulls to your lead cheek for cover, and the rear shoulder is hunched over your rear jaw line.
- Return the punch along the same path.

Lead hook

- To fire a proper hook, you must keep a 90 degree bend in your striking arm. Lock that elbow and do not allow it to extend upon impact.
- The punch will travel in a horizontal plane with the palm facing down for tight (inside) hooks and palm facing you for medium and long-range hooks.
- The punch is best executed by using the "door slamming" method.
- Think of your rear foot as a door hinge and the upper body as the door itself.

● Practice slamming the door without firing the hook to get used to the ballistic feel of the entire body that is needed for a powerful punch.

● Once the door slamming coordination has been acquired, add the hook. Concentrate on a horizontal path and maintaining a 90-degree arm angle.

● Upon impact, return the lead arm to cover position.

Rear hook

- Use the same considerations as the lead hook, but move the door hinge to your lead foot.

- Keep in mind that rear hooks should be used in combinations and preferably as the third link because they are fairly easy to read and counterpunch.

1
2
3
1
2
3

Lead uppercut

● The 90-degree angle rule applies to uppercuts, too. Any extension of the arm is wasted movement and will pull you out of position against a sharp puncher.

● To execute, dip approximately 8-10 inches with the lead knee and shoulder while angling your lead shoulder toward the opponent.

● At the same time drop your lead hand approximately six inches from shoulder level and turn your palm toward you.

● Stand up through the punch, snapping the lead hip forward and allowing your lead hand to travel no more than six inches above lead shoulder level.

● Return to position immediately.

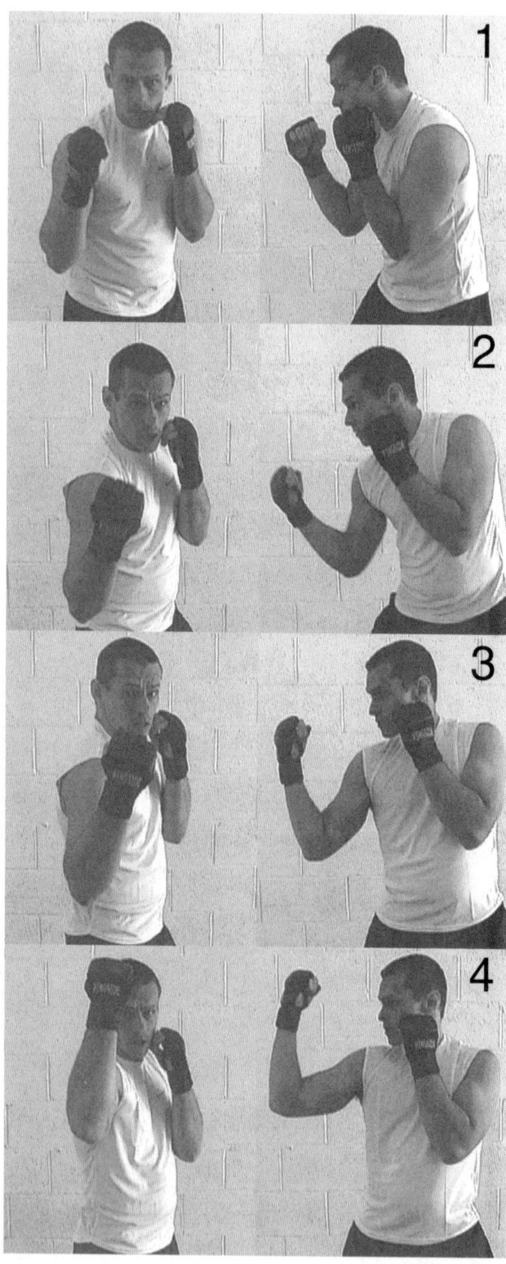

1
2
3
1
2
3

Rear uppercut

- Bend at the knees to dip your stance and turn the rear shoulder toward the opponent.

- To execute, follow the guidelines for the lead uppercut.

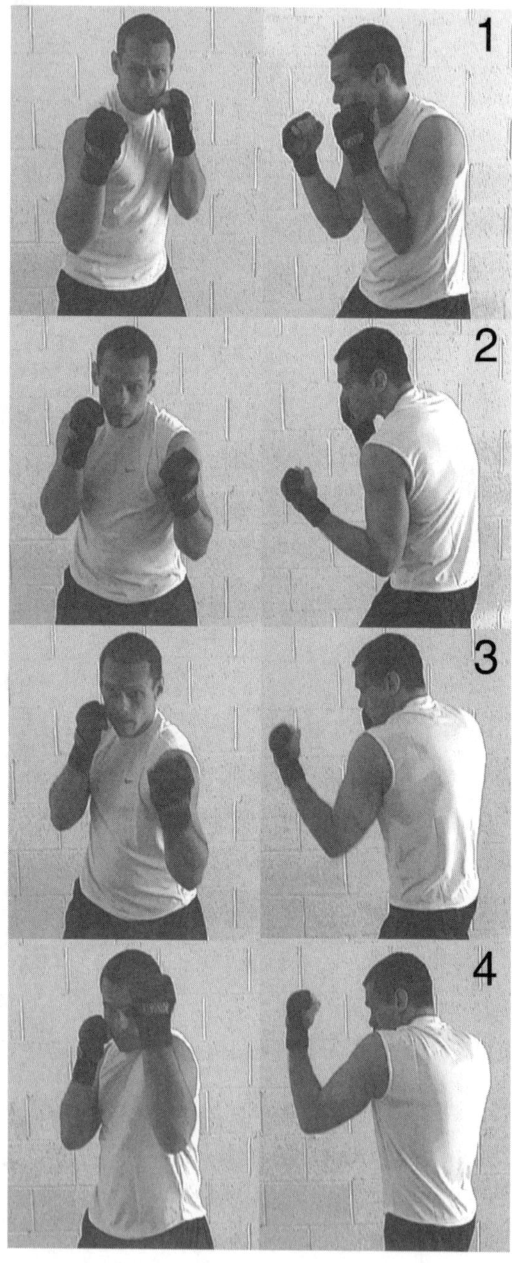

1
2
3
1
2
3

Rear overhand

- The rear hand shot from the standard boxing repertoire is rarely used, but definitely has its applications.
- The punch travels in a minor looping arc over an opponent's jab (or over his cross/rear straight if his lead does not match yours).
- To execute, use the body mechanics described for the cross, but as you fire the rear hand, visualize pitching a softball into the floor approximately six inches in front of your lead foot.
- Your hand is palm down.
- Return to position quickly because this punch opens you up as you throw it.

1
2
3
4
5

Body punching considerations

● You can and should fire all these punches to the body except for the rear overhand.

● Always lower your stance to the target level when throwing body shots. This allows you to put body mass into each shot (otherwise you are firing only arm punches) and gives you more reach than allowed when punching at a downward angle.

● Keep in mind that if you stay upright while throwing body shots, you will leave your head wide open for counterpunching.

3 Insertion shots

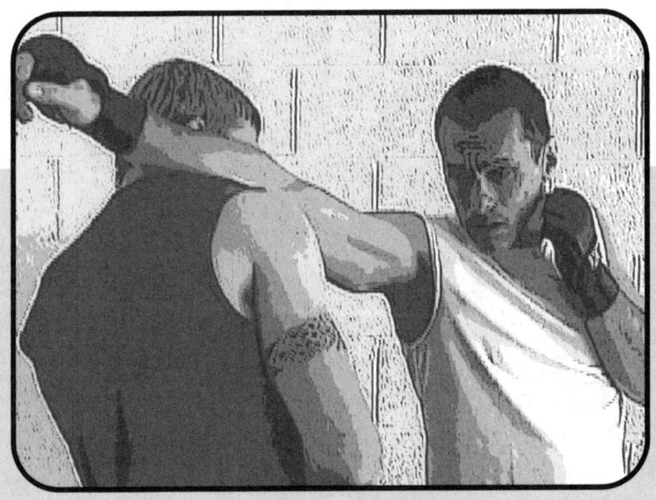

Insertion shots are strikes that are fired not as initial or primary blows but happen in either accidental or incidental avenues. By training them in an intentional manner, you will open up your "straight boxing" arsenal radically transforming it into an unpredictable and formidable NHB arsenal.

Louisville slugger

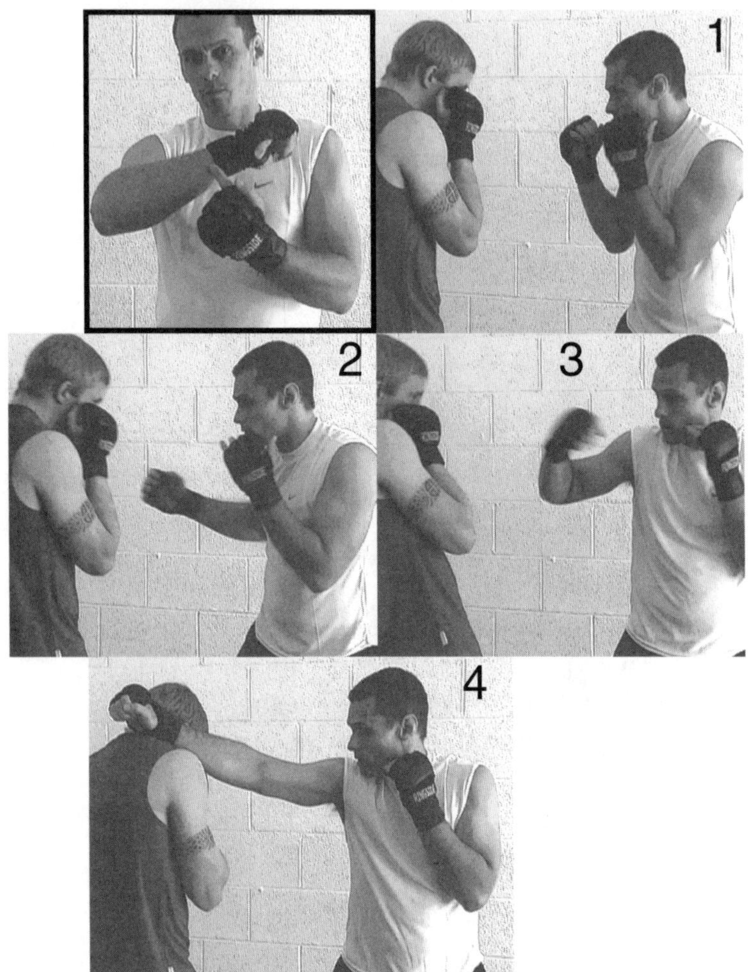

- This is a back forearm shot fired after your missed hooks.
- To execute, fire a lead (or rear) hook and upon missing (or after making contact) allow the forearm to whip out at a horizontal angle while returning to position.
- It is important to "whip" with the forearm and not "club."

Cram

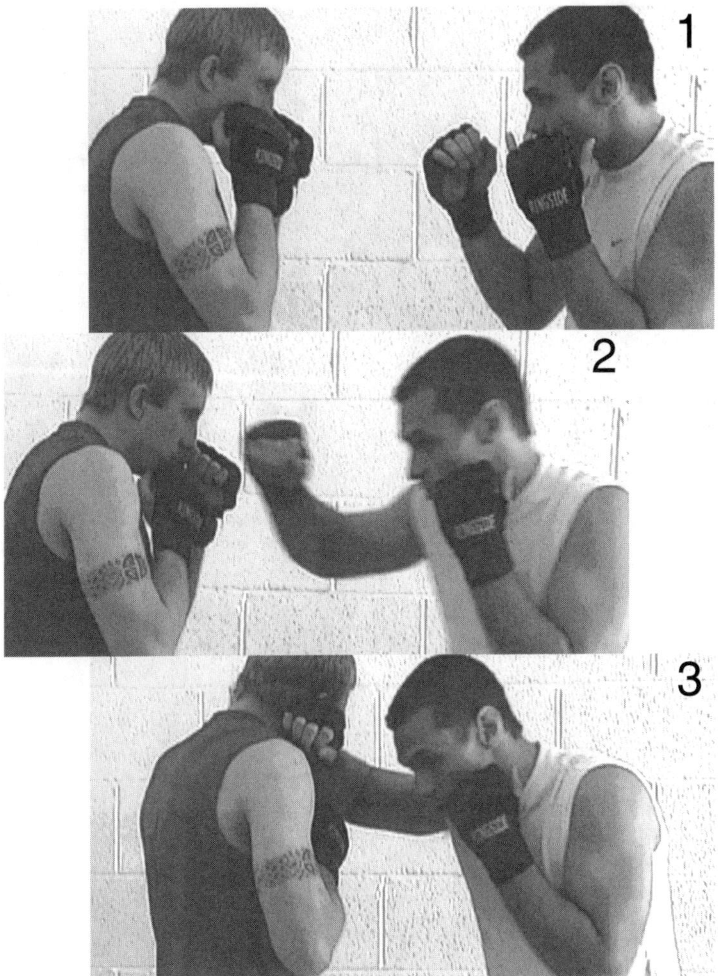

- A variant of the Louisville slugger.
- You are fighting inside and to make room you merely drive the outside edge of the lead forearm up and into your opponent's jaw.

Hammers

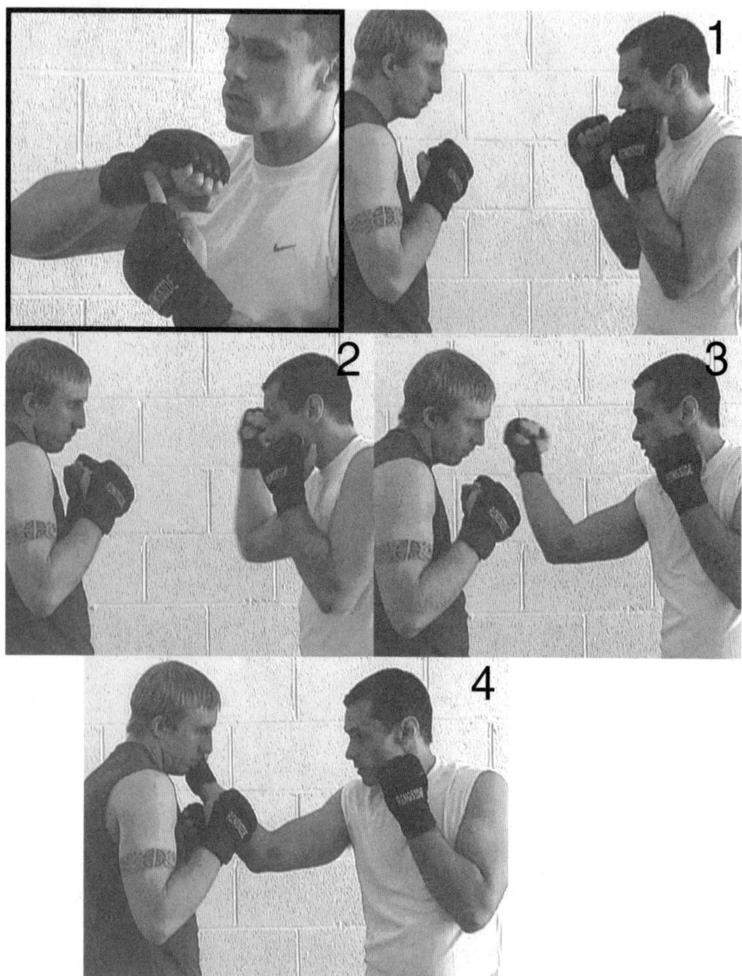

- Hammers are whipping blows delivered inside to medium range with the bottom or "hammer" surface of the closed fist.
- They are whipped with the added impetus of the door slamming mechanics used in firing hooks.
- Hammers are fired horizontally at the temple, jaw and side of the neck.

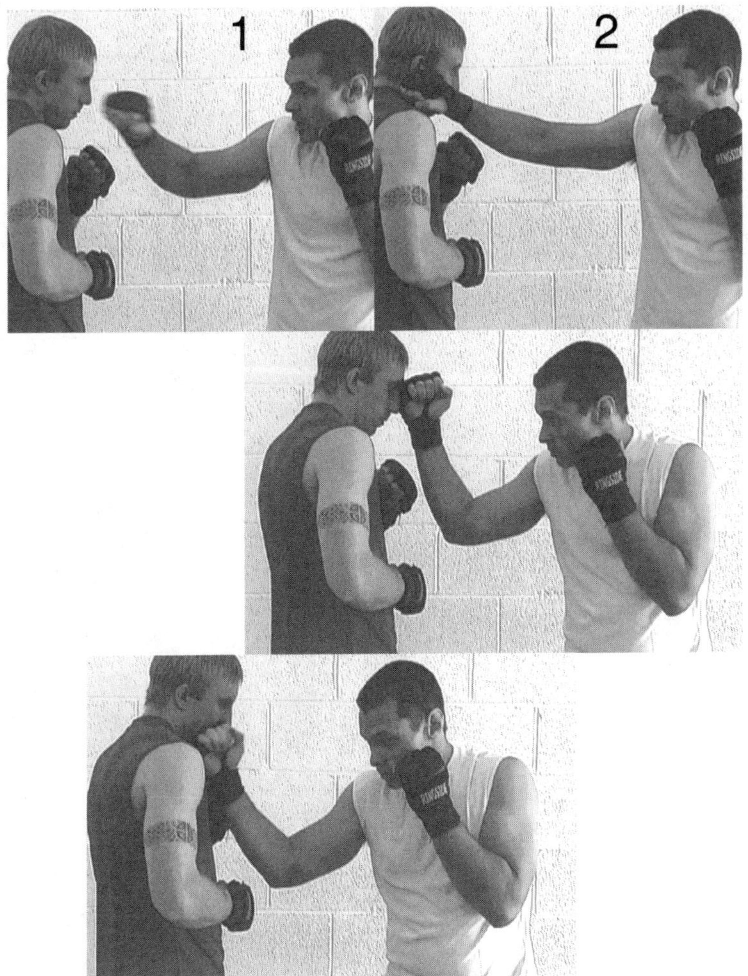

● And vertically at the nose, collarbone and back of the head of a bent-over opponent.

Battling nelson dig

● This is a horizontal hammer delivered against an opponent's short ribs (floating ribs) when in tight.

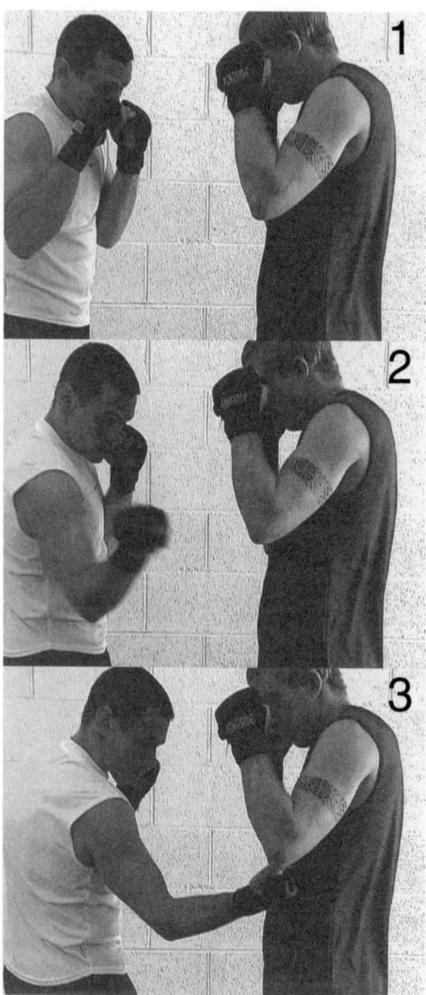

"Touch gloves" dirty trick

● A hammer also can be used in an aggressive touching of gloves at the beginning of a match in an effort to jam an opponent's fingers.

● I mention this as a warning only so it doesn't happen to you. I don't advocate its use, since I prefer the camaraderie of the sport over bad intentions.

Ax punches

- These are essentially long-range hammers. The required whipping motion entails the bend in the elbow.

- Axes are primarily used just inside the long-range game. They can be used horizontally and vertically.

- They are recommend only for targeting the head. The extended whipping and range of ax punches make their use on the body something to avoid.

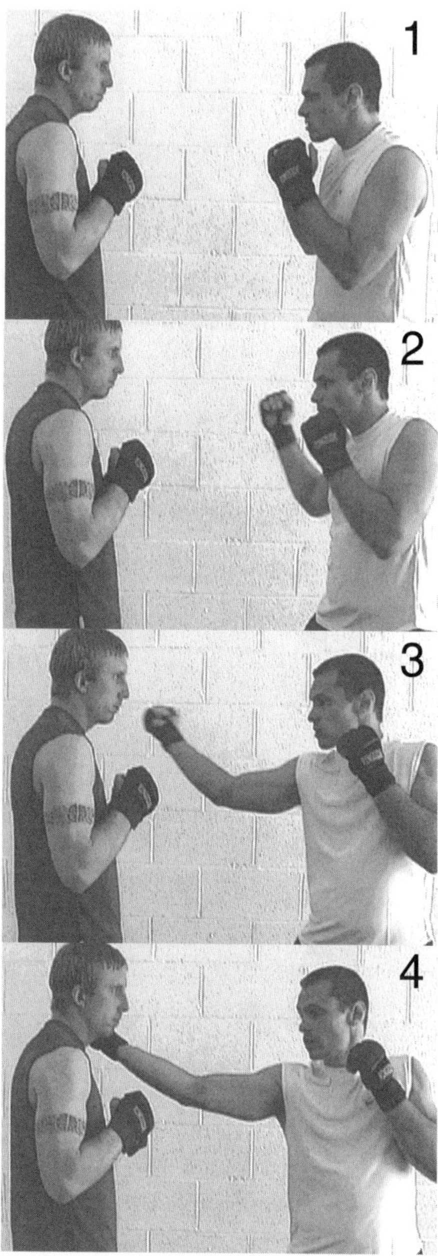

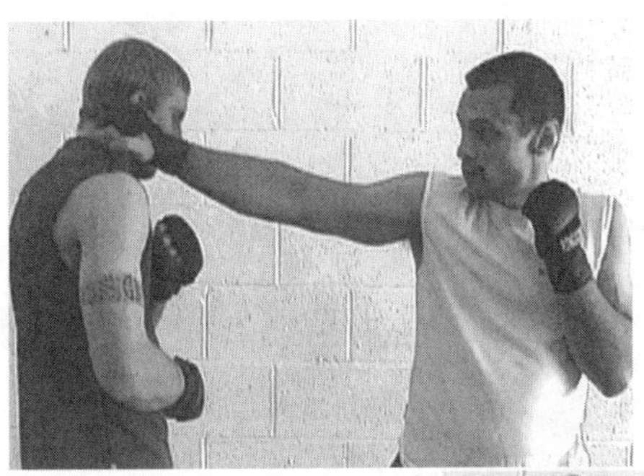

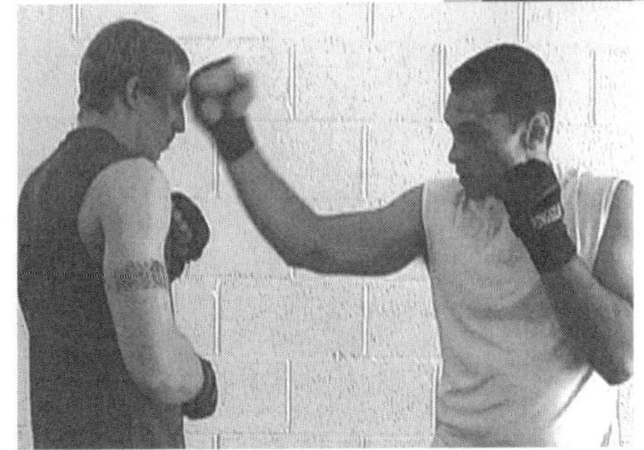

Hacksaws

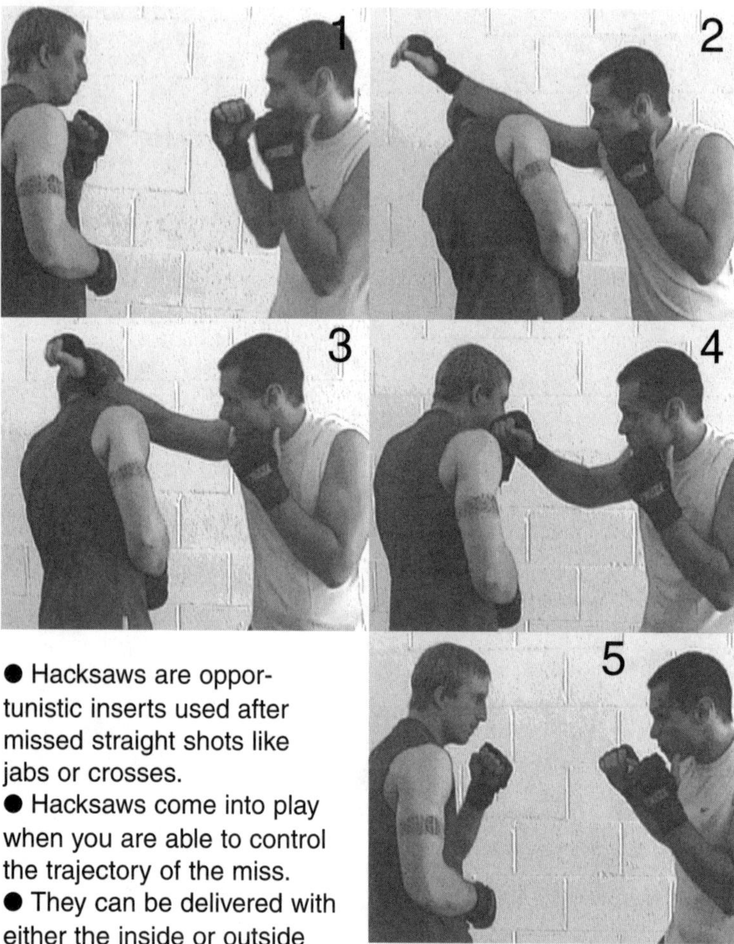

- Hacksaws are opportunistic inserts used after missed straight shots like jabs or crosses.
- Hacksaws come into play when you are able to control the trajectory of the miss.
- They can be delivered with either the inside or outside blade of the forearm.
- Once you realize that your punch has missed its mark, begin an immediate retraction to guard position.
- Allow the positive and/or negative motion of the missed punch to “saw” your forearm across an opponent’s head or neck.

4 Elbow work

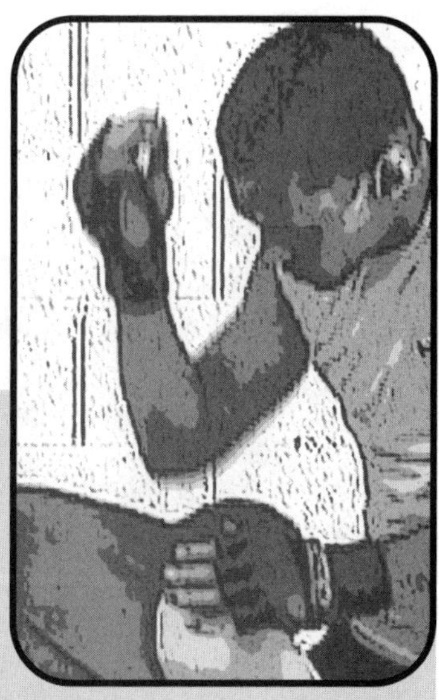

Elbows are excellent striking tools as demonstrated so ably and formidably in pure Muay Thai contests. It is difficult to find an NHB match that permits full use of the elbow arsenal (they are that damaging). We demonstrate the elbow arsenal primarily as self-defense, although each tool can be applied to an NHB situation in which the elbow's use is allowed.

Concepts to keep in mind when executing any elbow strike:

1. Strike with the elbow, not the forearm. Strive to make contact with the tip of the elbow for maximum effectiveness.

2. There is no need to wind up or execute door slamming techniques to make the elbow effective. Elbows are delivered most efficiently as an isolated movement of the arm rather than with the entire body.

3. If you are close enough to deliver an elbow, you are close enough to receive an elbow. With that in mind, always throw an elbow from the proper cover positions described.

Cross elbows

● Cross elbows are horizontal elbows delivered with either the lead or rear arm.

● To execute, lift your striking arm into a horizontal position with the fist and wrist relaxed. Clenching the fist or musculature of the forearm impedes the speed and adds nothing to the power of this strike.

● Raise your cover hand (nonstriking hand) and place the back of it on your forehead, palm facing the opponent. This protects

Cross elbows, both sides

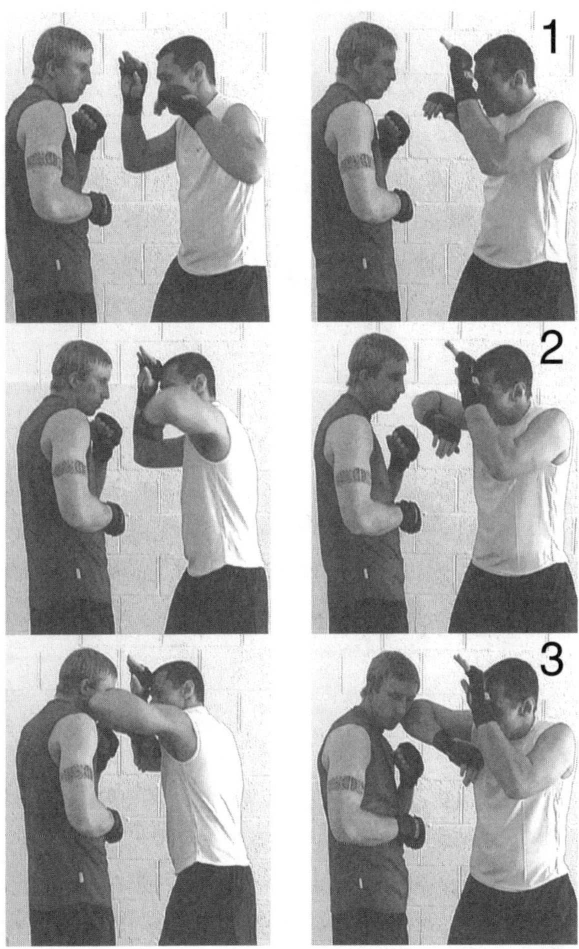

you from incoming elbows as you throw your own.

● Swing your striking arm at the shoulder joint with no waist twist and stop your momentum as the elbow reaches your mid-line (centerline).

● Return to guard position.

Up elbows

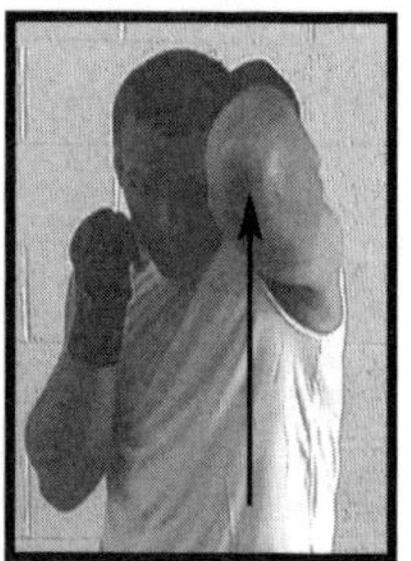

- Up elbows are analogous to uppercuts in the straight boxing arsenal.
- To deliver, relax your hand and lift the elbow straight up to the target area — usually the jaw or face of a crouching opponent.
- Return to guard position.
- To deliver an up elbow from the rear side, turn your waist so that the rear shoulder is facing your target before firing.

Down elbows

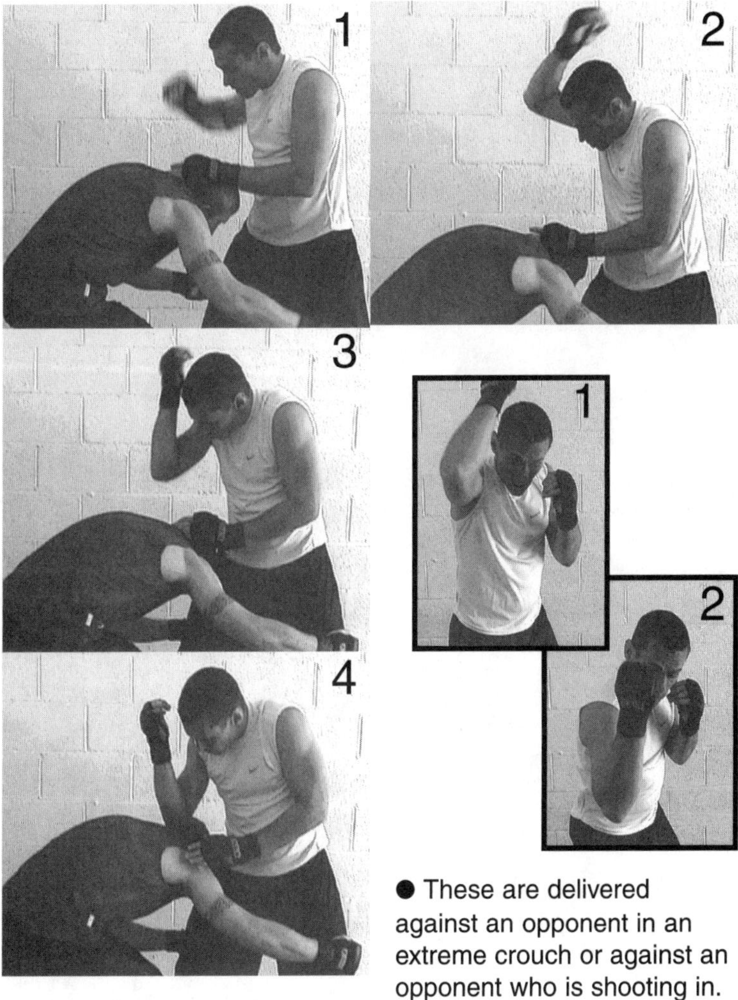

- These are delivered against an opponent in an extreme crouch or against an opponent who is shooting in.
- You must have good control of your base.
- The striking surface is the very tip of the elbow.
- The down elbow is the only elbow strike that uses body torque to assist its effectiveness.
- As you drop the elbow, contract your abdominal musculature to assist in the force of the strike.

Corkscrew elbows

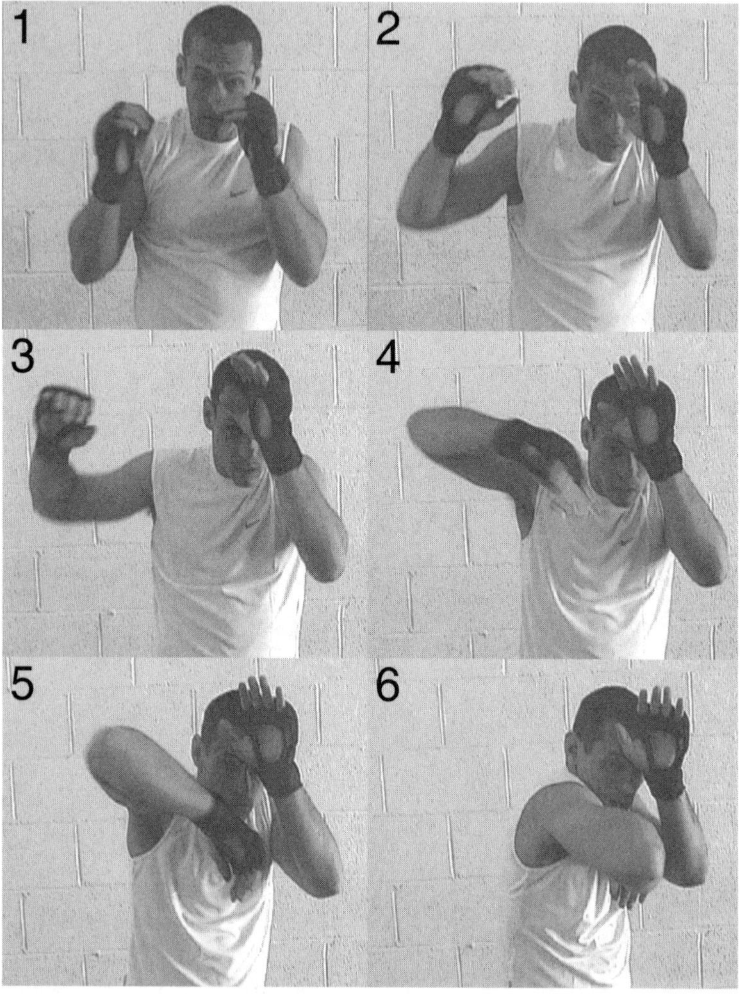

● The corkscrew is delivered much like the cross elbow, but the entry angle is different.

● Instead of traveling in a horizontal arc, the corkscrew elbow whips down at a 45-degree angle toward your midline (centerline) to catch the opponent in a downward arc/rip across the face.

Corkscrew action

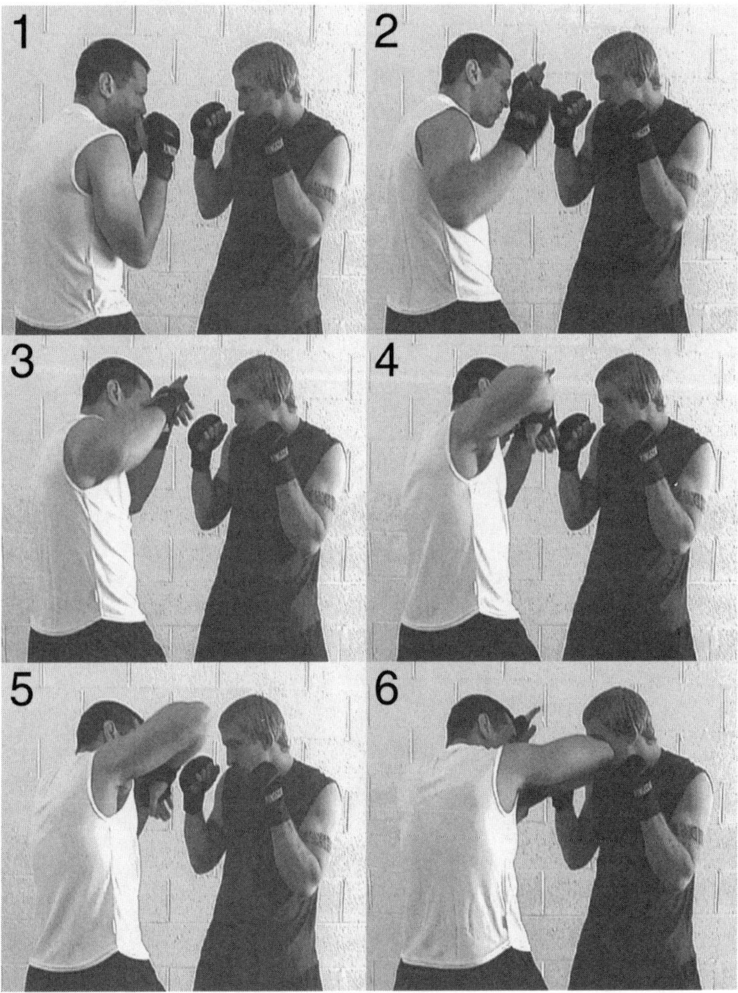

● The corkscrew is used primarily to enter between the twin parallel shells of an opponent's high stonewall cover.

Back elbows

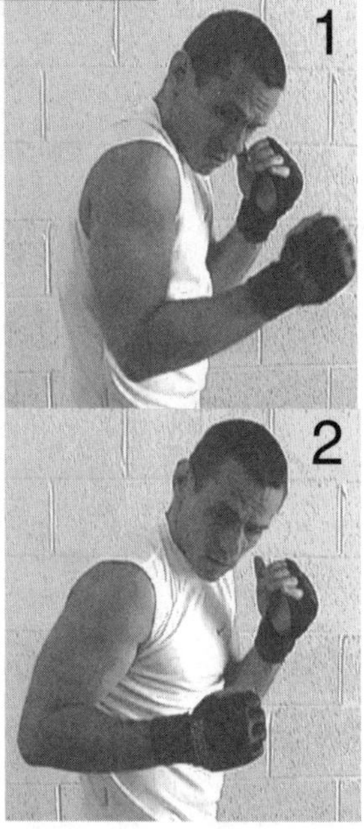

● Back elbows are not necessarily fight stoppers. They are effective aggravators when an opponent has your back.

● The back elbow is delivered with the rear tip of the elbow and can be vertical by firing straight back into an opponent's mid-section or horizontal by throwing back into an opponent's head.

Back elbows in action

5
Elbows as inserts

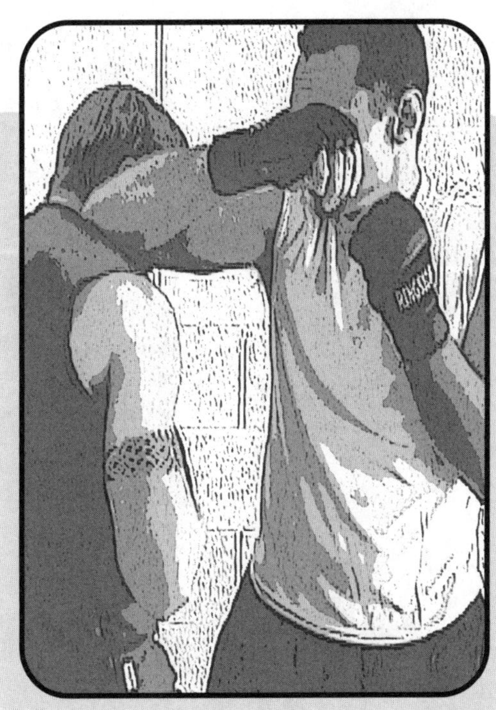

Elbows can be used in the insert manner of accidental or incidental application coupled with the straight boxing arsenal.

Cross elbow off a missed hook

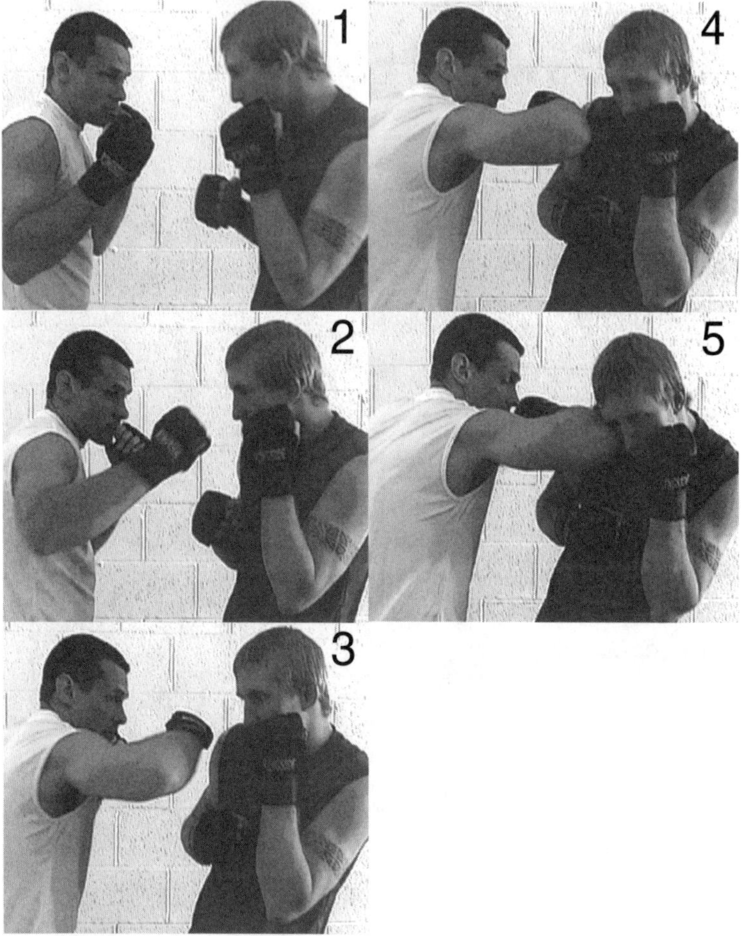

- You have fired a lead or rear hook and missed.

- By increasing the degree of bend in your elbow in a ballistic fashion — think bringing your fist toward your chest — you can use this same trajectory to deliver a cross elbow.

Up elbow off a missed uppercut

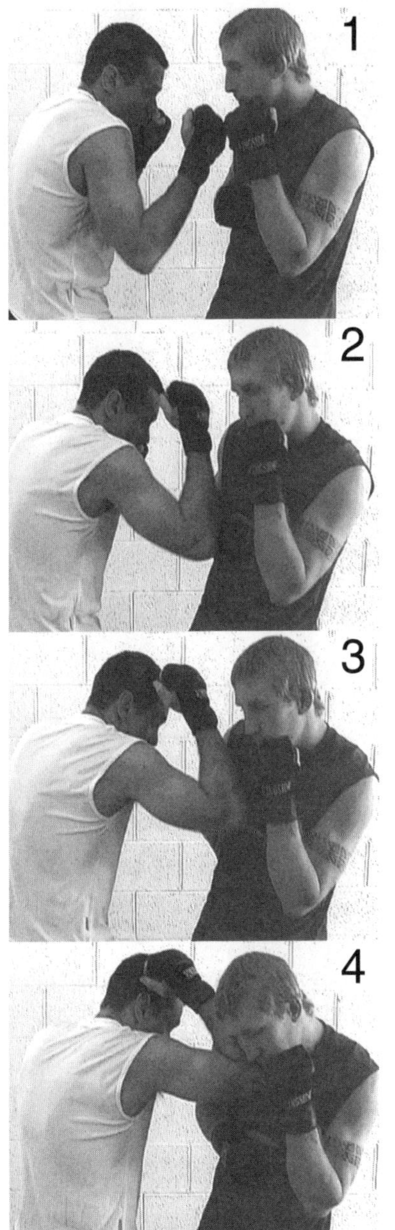

● Utilizing the same concept as the insert, once you miss with an uppercut, increase the angle of bend in your arm and strike with the elbow.

Back elbow off a missed hook

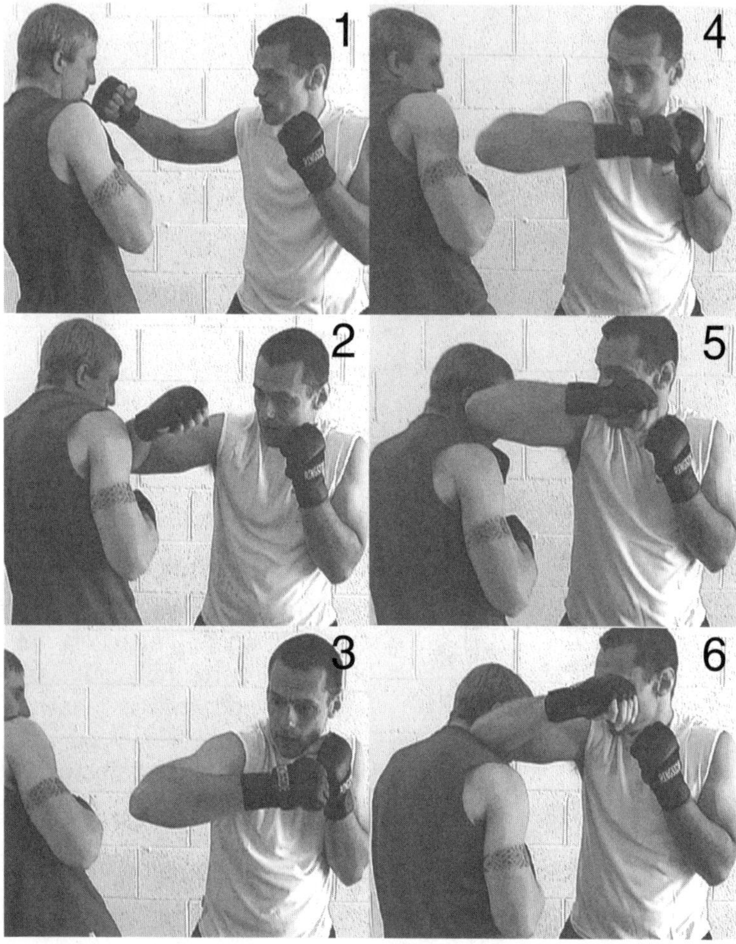

● You have missed another hook, but rather than executing the cross elbow off the same limb, turn it into a back elbow as you return the arm to guard position.

Straight boxing, insert, elbow combination ...

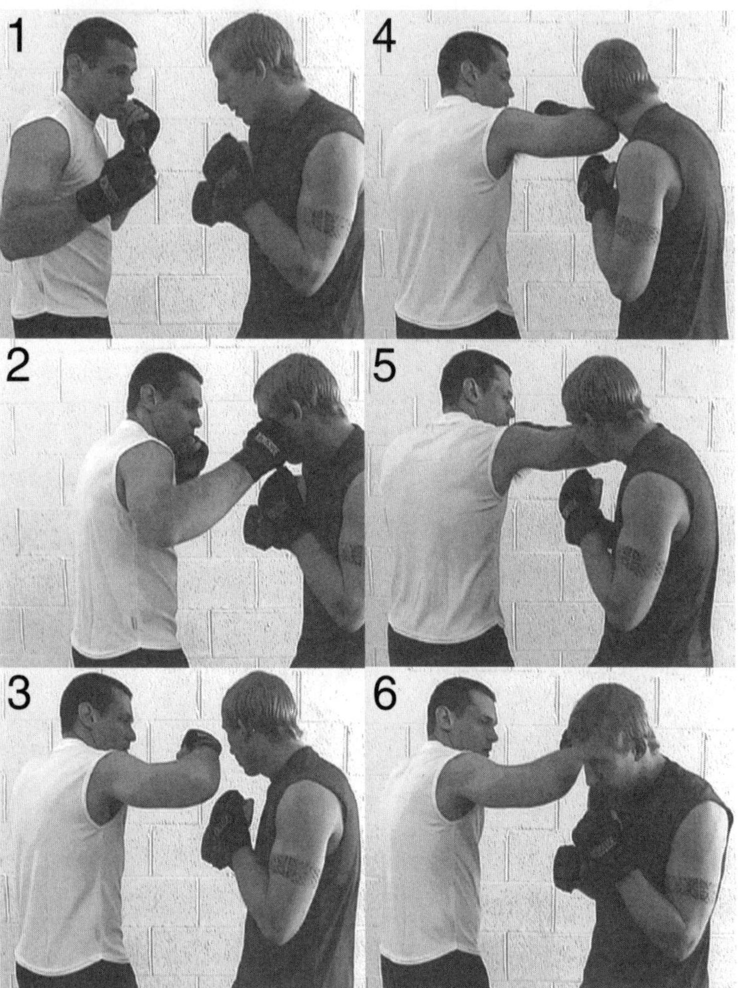

- All inserts can be combined in numerous fashions to create interesting straight boxing/insert/elbow combinations.

Example:

- Fire and land a lead hook.
- Increase the angle of bend and strike a second time with a cross elbow with the same limb.
- Back elbow with the same limb.

... still going ...

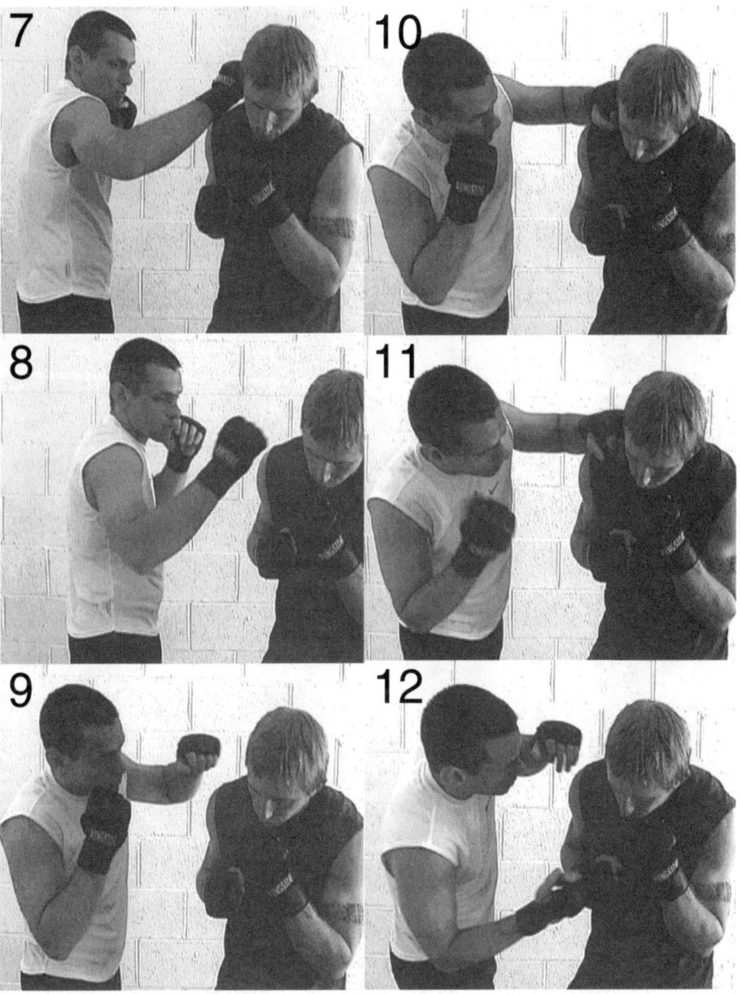

- Allow your arm to open in a ballistic manner to deliver a back hammer blow.
- Follow that with a rear cross.

More →

... and combo finale

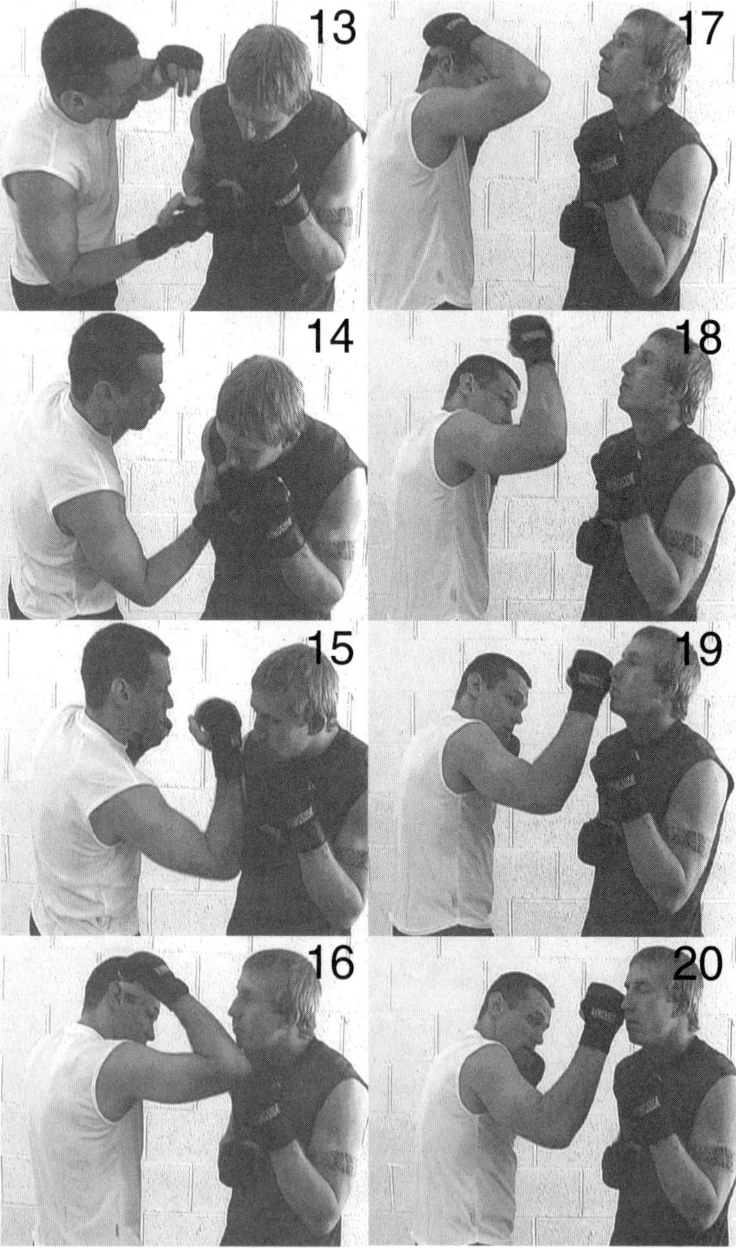

- Followed by a lead uppercut.

- Increase the elbow angle to follow through with a lead up elbow with the same limb.

- Bring the up elbow back to guard quickly while delivering a downward hammer with the same hand.

- This eight-point combination fires three straight boxing shots, three elbows and two inserts. These concepts and combinations can be arranged many ways.

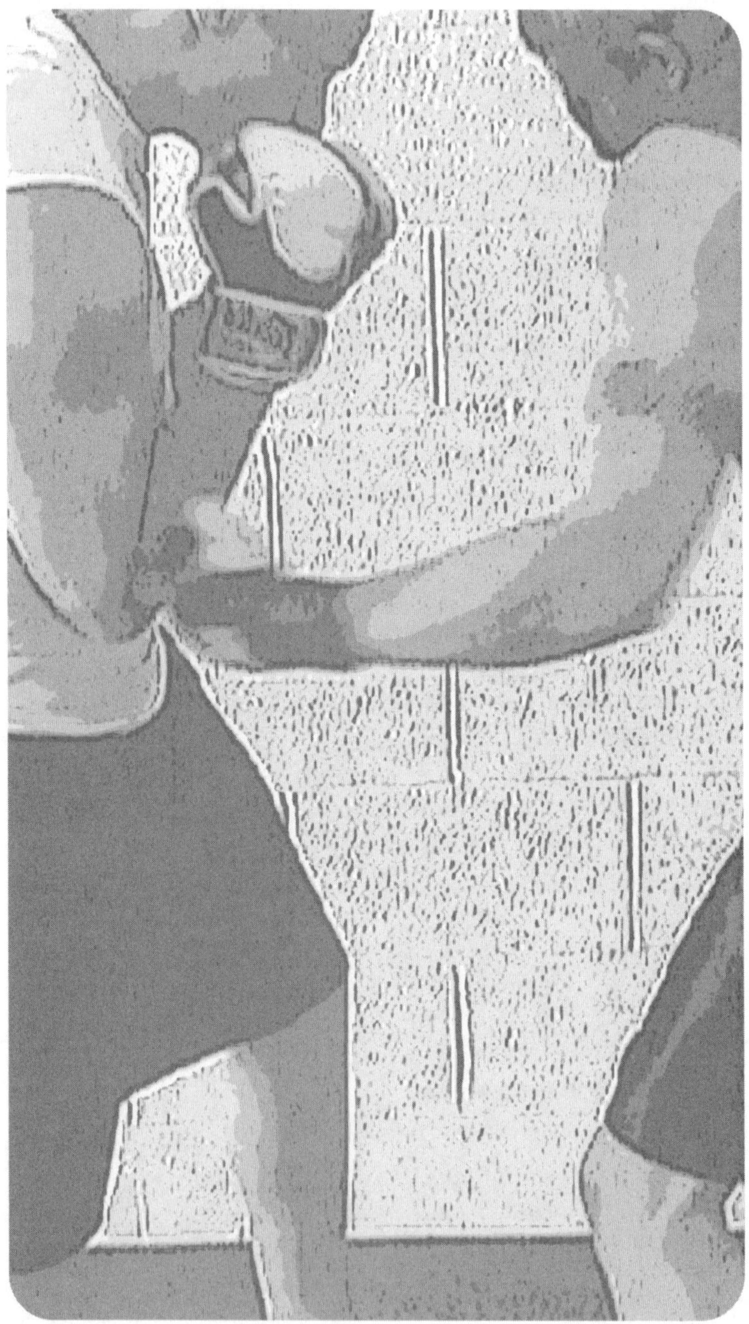

6
Low blows

You will be hard pressed to find NHB events that allow groin shots (thank God!), but if you do, here are a couple of hand strikes that can be used. These are also excellent self-defense strikes.

Low uppercut

● Use the same mechanics as the straight boxing uppercut, but strike the groin with the inner-wrist as opposed to the fist (cups are hard and can damage hands).

Slapper

1

2

3

- This shot is used inside a half-clinch and is foul beyond belief.
- Fire a low uppercut and allow your glove to catch the rear of the opponent's cup.
- Drag your striking hand up his body bringing the bottom edge of his cup along with you.
- Release to allow the elastic to fire that cup back into position. Ouch!

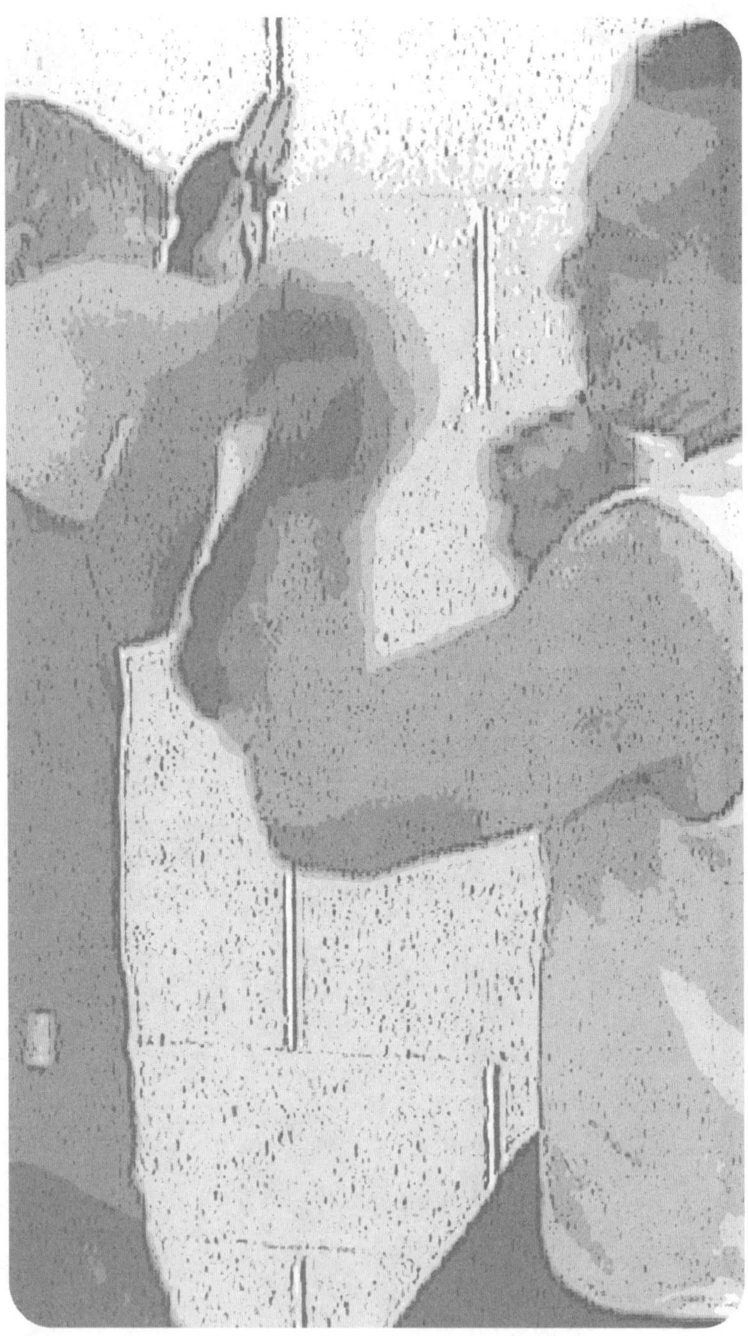

7 Straight self-defense strikes

These shots are for self-defense purposes only and have no place in any sportive NHB environment.

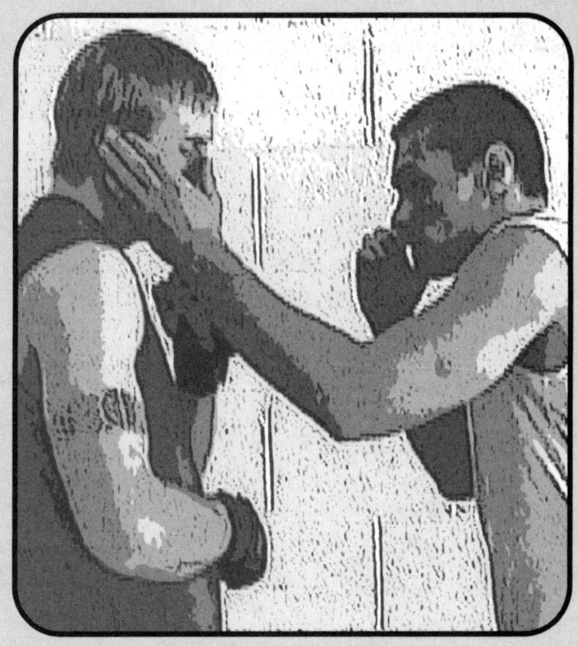

Thumbing

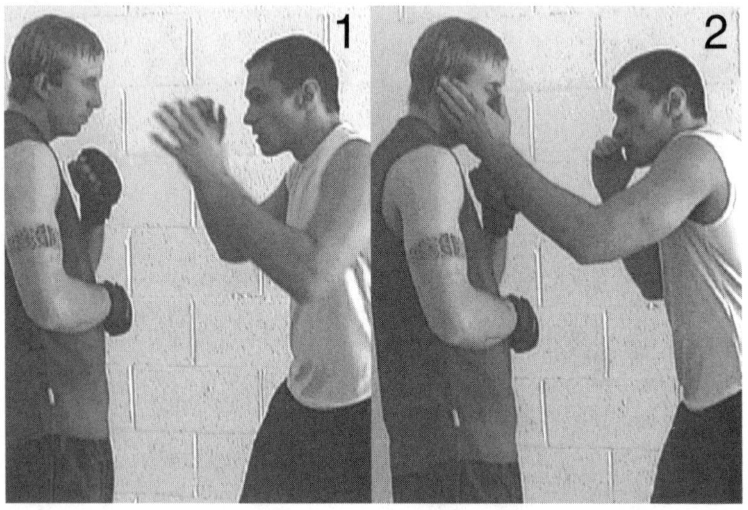

● You can use the thumbs in open-hand strikes to the eyes or eye gouging when fighting inside.

Finger jabs / spears

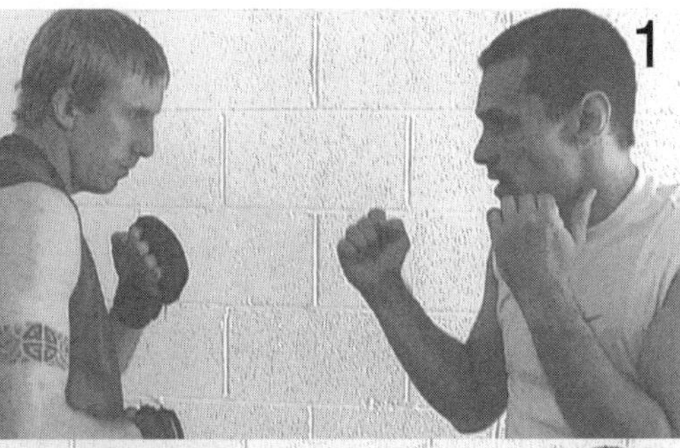

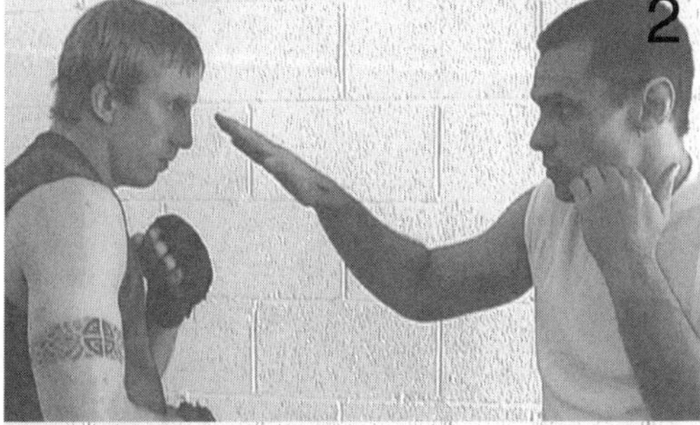

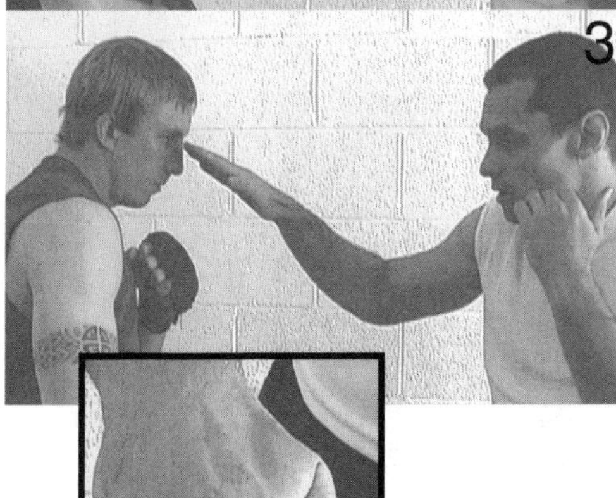

- Like throwing the jab, but instead of using the fist, strike with the fingertips. The target is the eyes.

- To provide greater stability for the fingers that have a tendency to give in the extended position, stack your fingers in this manner: Cross the index and ring fingers in front of your middle finger allowing the crossed fingers to meet at the fingertips. Squeeze them together tightly.

Throat work

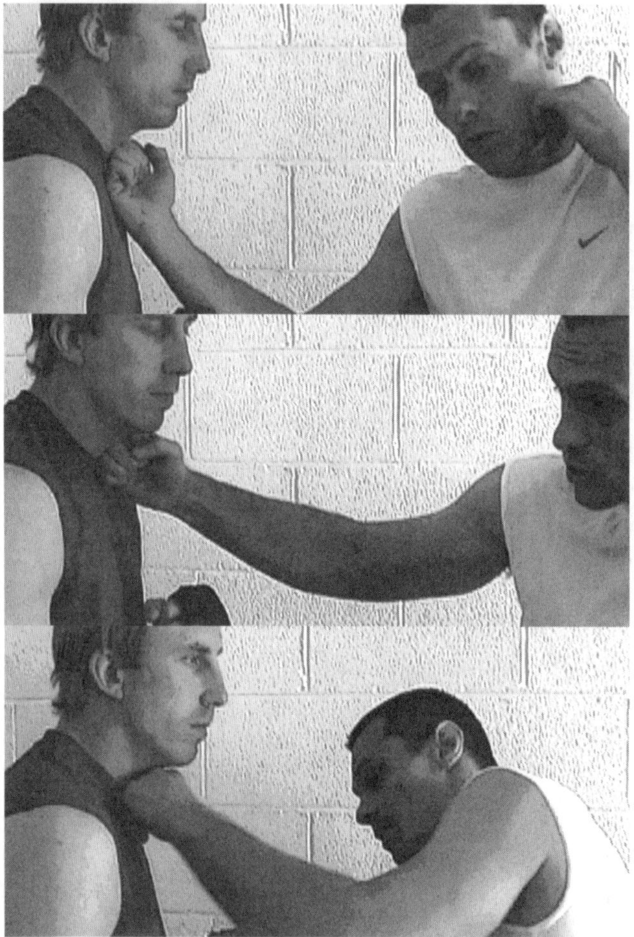

● The human throat is an excellent target in self-defense situations. Use the straight boxing arsenal, insert tools and elbow weapons for formidable results.

C hand strikes

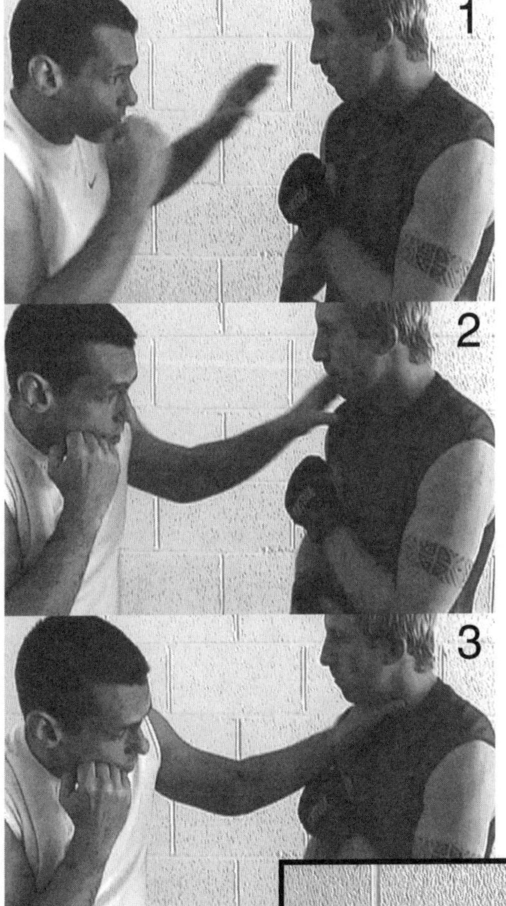

● You can also successfully strike the throat with **C** hand strikes.

● Open your hand to form a rigid letter **C.** Use the web between the thumb and index finger as a striking surface against the throat.

● Fire the **C** hand shot with the same mechanics used for straight punches.

8
Head butts

At one time, head butts were relatively common in NHB competition. Now you are hard pressed to find this weapon permitted (probably for the sport's best interests). The following tools are provided for competitions where this is still permissible and for self-defense work.

Strike surface

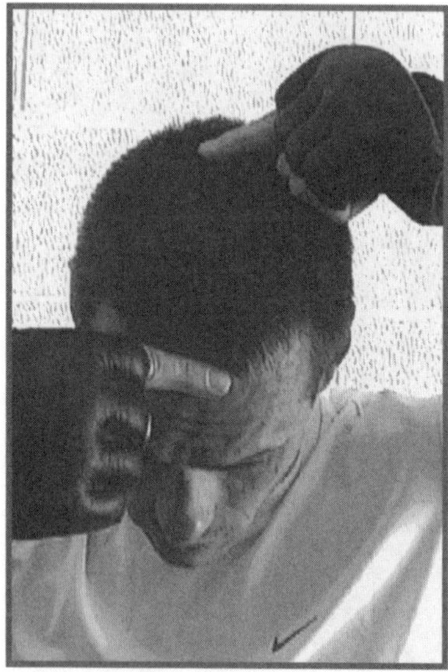

Do not strike with your forehead but rather with the top of your head above your hairline. The reasons are twofold: The top of the head is a stronger surface. The scalp cuts easily. Chances are good that if you strike someone with a healthy head butt, you will cut and bleed (although not as much as your opponent). By striking above the hairline, you are allowing potential cuts to coagulate in the hair and bleed toward either side of the head rather than into the eyes. (This rule even holds for the head-shaven or follically challenged.)

Bad butt

Free head butt

- This head butt launched without benefit of a clinch is fired from close quarters.
- It is best delivered after a setup (a short jab or lead hook, for example).
- To execute, drop your base (bend the knees) and fire up and into your opponent using your legs as the driving musculature, not the neck muscles, to snap you into position. By firing with the legs you put more mass into the strike. Ballistic snaps of the neck muscles may cause you injury.

Clinch head butt

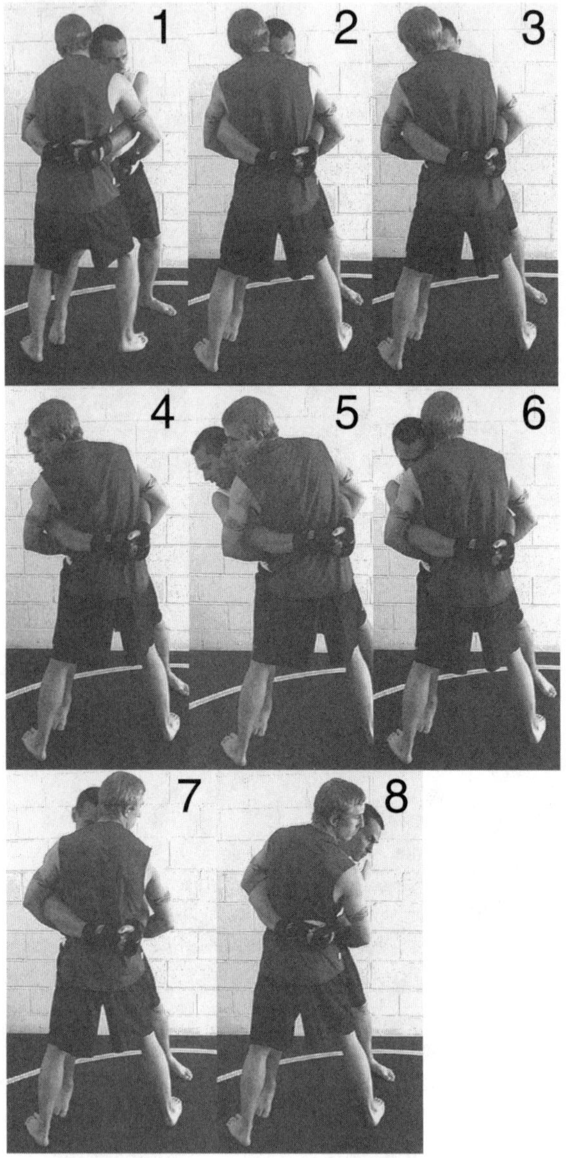

● In a loose clinch, this head butt can be delivered with the top of the head by dipping at the knees and standing up into your opponent.

● If the clinch is tight, you can "wag" the head butt into position. To execute the wag, turn your head so that you are driving as much skull as you can manage into your opponent's face. The leg drive is not used because balance comes into consideration in a tight clinch.

False clinch head butt

- This is a hard-hitting shot fired off your attempted body-lock (clinch).

- If you have one hand around your opponent's waist, grip the waistband at the back of his trunks (here the right hand grips).

- Place the palm of your other hand against his near shoulder.

- Dip your legs putting the top of your head just under his jaw.

● To fire this strike, perform the following three motions simultaneously:

1. Pull his waistband.

2. Push his shoulder (these motions start him in a half-spin).

3. Stand up launching a head butt through his jaw.

9 Clinch inserts

Since we've addressed clinches with head butts, let's look at a few insert strikes that are designed specifically for clinch work.

Poppers

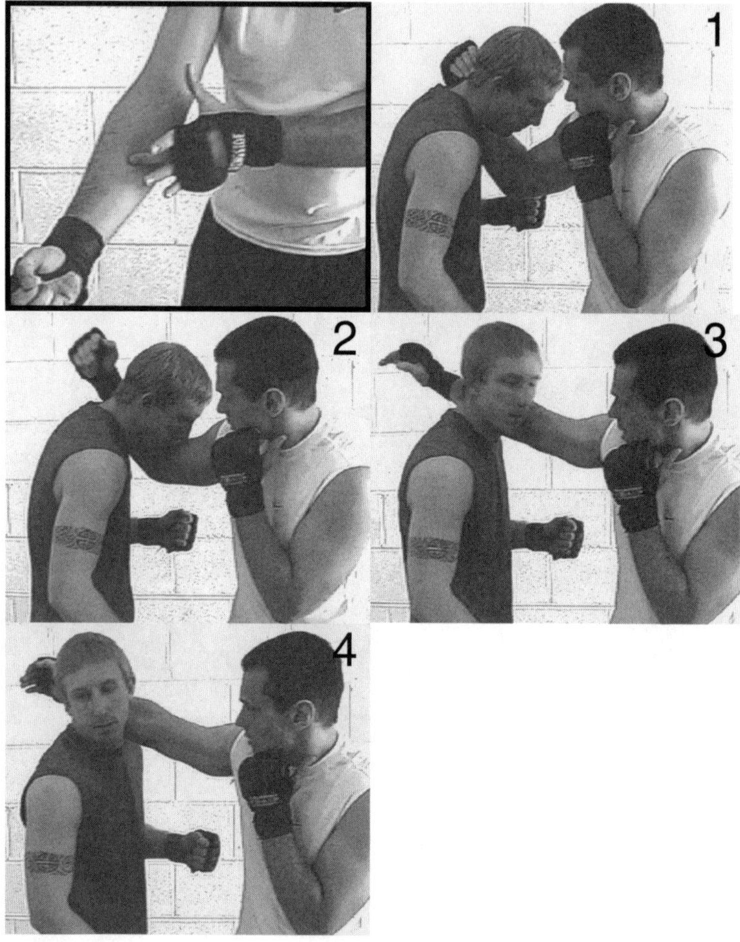

- Poppers are strikes using the inside crook of your arm in a unique manner.
- Poppers carry a deceptive amount of force. Use them with care.
- Do not merely club with the inner arm, but fire in the described manner:
- Grip the nape of the opponent's neck tightly with your hand.
- In a ballistic manner, extend the right arm allowing your inner elbow to strike your opponent in the side of the head.

Poppers as setups

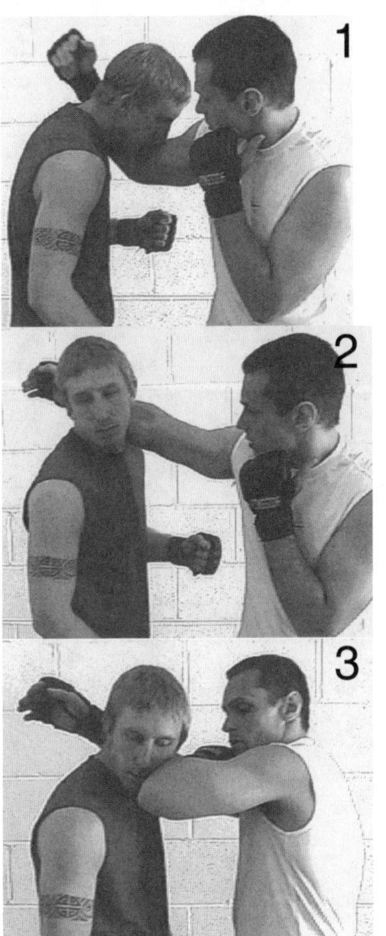

- Poppers are ideal striking weapons for follow-up strikes.

Example:

- Pop your opponent with your right arm sending his head directly into a left cross elbow.
- The cross elbow will return the head to your right hand. You gain control and the possibility of another popper.

Upward shrug

● Shrugs are short jarring strikes with the shoulder. They are used to create movement in the clinch or as setups.

● The upward shrug is used inside a tight clinch. To execute, position your shoulder beneath the opponent's jaw and fire your shoulder upward.

Advancing shrug

● This variety is used in a loose clinch. To execute, grip the nape of your opponent's neck with your hand and launch your shoulder toward his chin while pulling his head into the strike.

Shrugs as setups

- Shrugs can set up inside weapons as in the following example.
- Strike an opponent with an advancing shrug.
- Use a popper off the same side arm to send his head to your left.

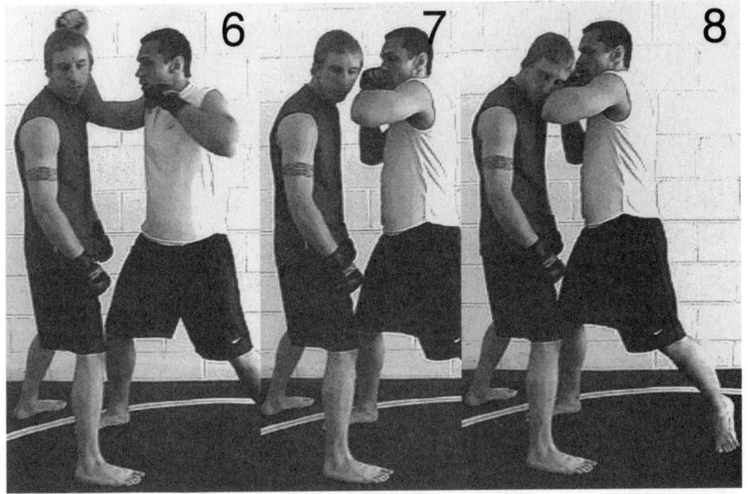

- Strike with a left cross elbow.
- Pull his head back in for another shoulder strike on the right side to repeat the cycle if you choose.

Cooker

- Cookers are used inside tight clinches to aggravate an opponent.
- Simply cover his mouth and nose with the palm of your hand.
- This is very disconcerting to an opponent especially after he has exerted himself.

Straight stomp

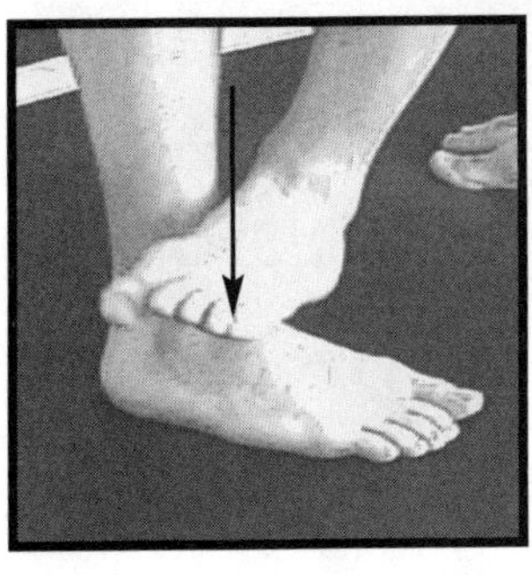

- Foot stomps are excellent clinch weapons.
- Use the opposite foot versus opposite foot orientation or right versus left and vice versa. Using same side feet (left versus left or right versus right) can upset your stance too much, which gives your opponent an opportunity to take your back.
- Strike with your heel against the juncture of his foot where the instep meets the ankle.
- Allow the heel to chop in and slide down his shin.

Shove stomp

● Perform the straight stomp and, if the opportunity permits, keep your weight on top of his foot.

● Break the clinch and shove him away while keeping your weight on his foot. This creates the potential for ankle damage.

High stepper

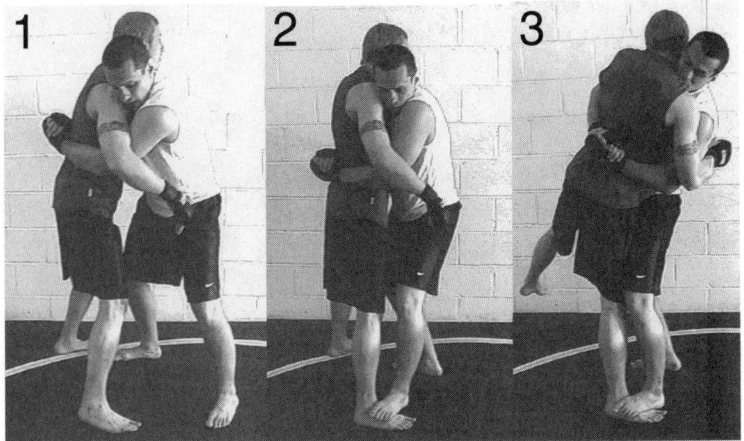

● Perform the straight stomp, but rather than breaking the clinch and shoving away, body lock the opponent and attempt to lift him while keeping your weight on his foot. This could cause ligament separation.

10 Clinch breakers

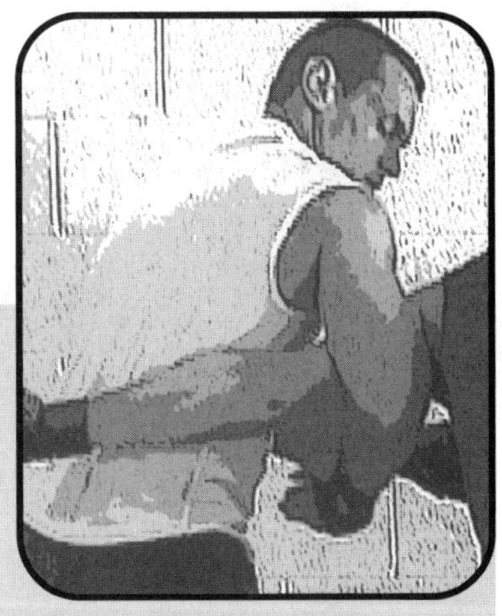

Clinches are energy-consuming endeavors. It is best to go on the offensive with directed energy once inside the clinch rather than using clinches to provide yourself or an opponent the opportunity to rest. As a general rule, if you have control of the clinch there is no need to break it, since it presents greater opportunities to strike or execute a takedown or even a standing submission. So, on the flip side, if you are on the bad side of clinch control, a few strategies for breaking clinches are needed.

Breaking clinches is not the same as controlling clinches. Collar-and-elbow pummeling, under- and overhooking, low-level pummeling, biceps riding, tie-up work and the like are excellent methods for learning clinch control. (Clinch control techniques could fill an entire book).

Here we seek to break the clinch, which means to leave it. Provided are two methods of inflicting potential damage while exiting and one way to create distance in a safe manner.

Overhook snap

- An opponent has a loose body-lock clinch (his arms are under yours).
- Overhook one of his arms just above the elbow (here the right arm overhooks the opponent's left arm).
- Turn to your left with force attempting to wrench his left elbow with a right overhook.

Underhook snap

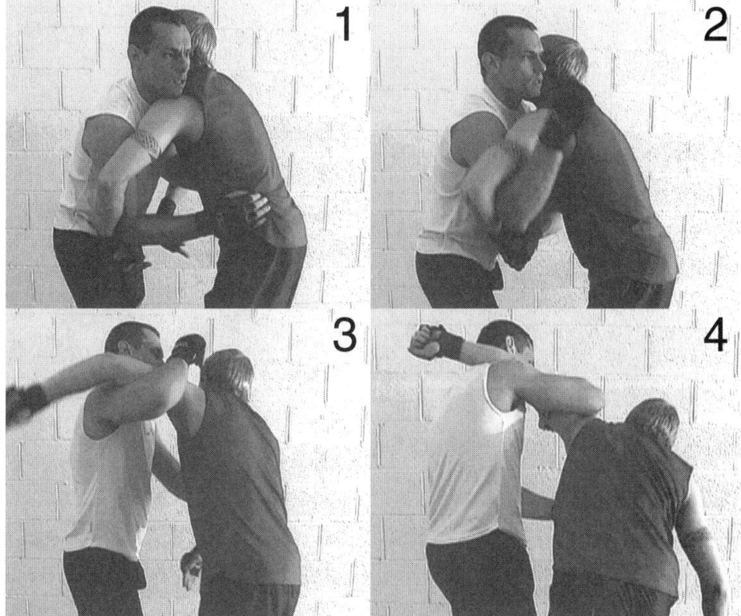

- Your opponent's arms are overhooking yours in an attempt to muffle your strikes.
- Underhook one of his controlling arms (in this case the right arm underhooks the opponent's left arm).
- Like the previous technique, turn to your left and forcefully attempt to wrench his left elbow with an underhook.

Bump

- The bump breaks a clinch allowing you to return to a striking game rather than a clinch control game.

- To execute, stack your palms on top of each other in the center of your opponent's chest.

- Bump the top of your head into the back of your stacked palms and use your entire body mass to get him moving.

- Extend your arms leaving them crossed at the wrist to defend against incoming strikes. Be sure to keep shoulders hunched and your face down in the gap between your biceps.

- Use retreating footwork once you initiate the bump to gain the distance desired.

11 Leg work

Now we introduce the recommended lower-body arsenal keeping in mind the upper-body weapons bias. This arsenal is slim when compared to the upper-body arsenal, but it is formidable in its own right and should be practiced diligently.

Purring kick

- Purring kicks originated in a masochistic tavern game played by Irish and Welsh miners. The participants would hold on to each other's shoulders and take turns kicking each other in the shins while wearing heavy brogans until one of the competitors would drop his hands away from his opponent's shoulders signifying defeat.
- Purring kicks can be executed with either the lead or rear foot. The striking surface is the inside of the heel, not the arch of the foot as it may appear.
- The kick should be executed only inside the clinch so your base is not compromised.
- It is used as a distraction weapon or to work an already damaged shin.
- The ideal target is the inner surface of the shin as opposed to the front or outside surfaces of the shin.
- To execute, fire your attacking foot (here the left) toward the target with toes facing the target.
- Turn your toes to the outside, snapping your heel into the opponent's shin at the very moment of impact.

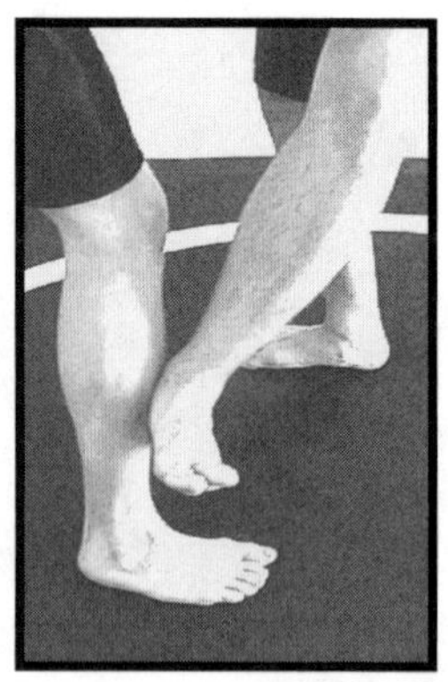

Grater

● The grater is a purring variant in which you strike with a purring kick high on an opponent's shin. Then allow your foot to remain in contact with his shin as you scrape it down the shin into a foot stomp.

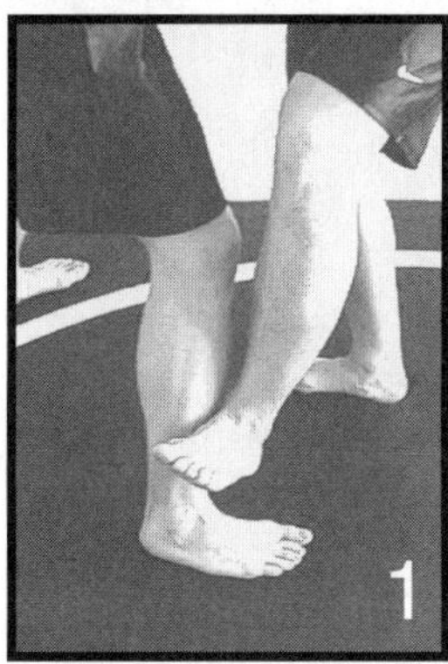

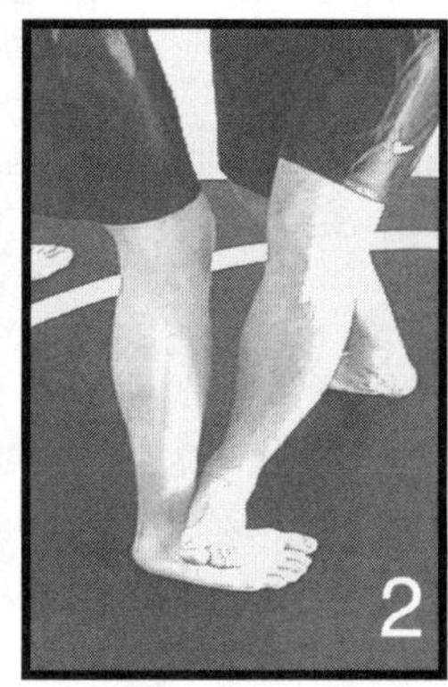

Thigh kick

- The thigh kick, a hallmark of Muay Thai, cannot be improved upon. It is a deceptively punishing weapon and most useful in the hands of a skilled competitor.

- We describe only the rear thigh kick. The lead or switch kick variants call for too much base shift and take the emphasis away from the upper-body weapons.

- To execute (shown here being fired with the left leg) step 45 degrees forward and toward your right with your right foot. The step allows you to put more mass into the shot and puts you in kicking range. (If you are close enough to fire the kick with no step, a hand attack would be more efficient and allows for faster combinations.)

- Turn the left point of your pelvis to face your opponent — it is important that the pelvis advance before the leg. It is the wind up or whip of the attacking leg that gives the strike its punishing power and not the hinging of the knee as found in Korean systems or Savate.

- Whip your hips and upper body hard toward the right. This allows slamming of the door to whip your striking leg into the target.

- Return to position immediately while controlling your momentum, so that a miss does not pull you off base or even worse, turn you 360 degrees.

- The striking surface of the kick is the shin — two inches above your ankle and 8 inches below your knee.

- Your target area is the outside of an opponent's thigh. Aim approximately four inches above his knee and eight inches below his hip joint. This is where the strike will be most effective.

1
2
3
4
5
6

More thigh kick

12 Knees

Knees are high-percentage stopping weapons and should be worked diligently. Their use outside of the clinch is debatable, but inside the clinch knees are formidable.

Straight knee

● The straight knee is fired with the rear knee, without benefit of a clinch. ● It is delivered in a straight trajectory as if you are punching with the knee. ● It is best delivered when the opponent has his back to the cage wall or ropes because your mass commitment makes his chances of side-stepping the strike unlikely. ● To execute, fire the point of your rear knee straight toward your opponent. ● Punch your hips toward him at the moment of impact. ● The target area is usually the midsection. Any higher and your base can be compromised without a clinch to stabilize yourself.

Up knee

● The up knee is best fired once you have at least one hand on an opponent.

● The rear knee fires in an upward arc with the hips punching through at the moment of impact.

13 Clinch knees

Clinch knees are, unquestionably, the most effective lower-body weapons. They can be fired from any kind of clinch, controlled or chaotic. Here, we describe an optimum clinch from which to fire the knees and the ideal manner to execute.

Optimum clinch

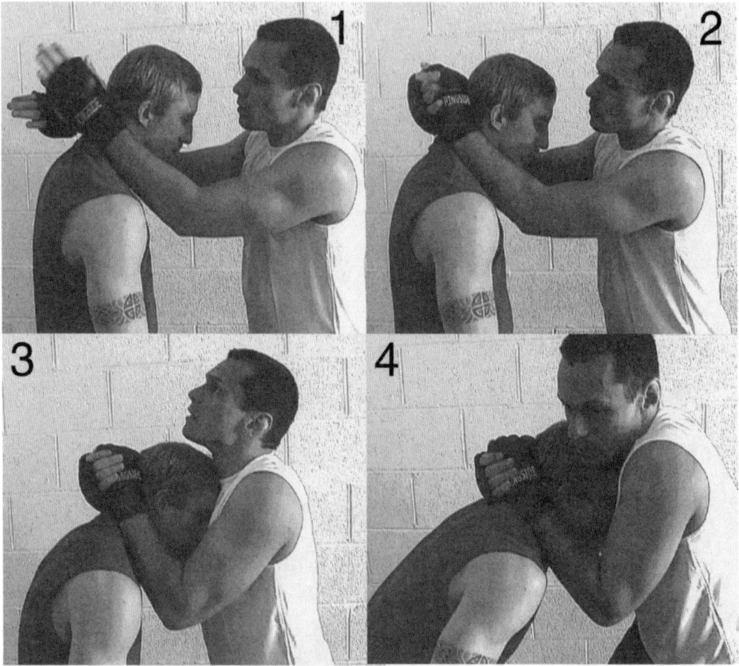

● Clasp your hands in a palm-to-palm grip behind the opponent's neck. Do not interlace fingers because they can be broken easily.

● Squeeze your forearms together and hold them in a tight grip. The most common clinching mistake is applying zero pressure with the forearm grip.

● Drop your hips back and place the opponent's forehead on your upper chest.

● Once his head is posted on your chest, drop your hips back even more and apply downward pressure to the back of his neck so that his nose is forced into your chest and his jaw and throat are exposed.

● It's from this position that you fire the clinch knee.

Optimum clinch with clinch knee strikes

Alternating clinch straight knees

● Perform the optimum clinch and fire your rear knee straight into the opponent. ● Punch your hips and jerk his head at the moment of impact to amplify the damage. ● Step the foot of the kicking leg to the mat and step/skip your lead foot to the rear.

● Fire your rear knee into your opponent. ● Continue changing footwork in this manner. ● An alternate target is the head. The knee travels in an upward arc toward the face rather than punching at the midsection.

Final offensive note: Clinch round knee

I will not introduce this clinch knee weapon because its side-stepping footwork can compromise your base.

It is undoubtedly a formidable weapon in straight striking contests but its statistical value is negligible in NHB.

For those who wish to add it to their arsenal, see the Resources section for recommendations of Muay Thai texts.

Well, there you have it — a little over 50 NHB striking tools. Next, we look at high-percentage defenses against many of these weapons so that your defensive arsenal is prepared to cope with a varied offensive attack.

NHB striking defense

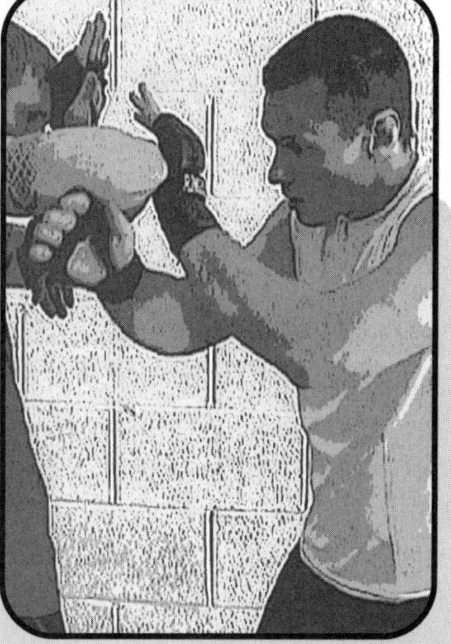

It's just as important, if not more so, to be a good defensive player as it is to be a good striker. Having dynamite in each fist and TNT in every elbow and knee is all for naught if you are "taking two to give your one." What follows is a comprehensive defense system for the NHB athlete. Please remember to practice these techniques as diligently as the striking arsenal.

It is easy to overlook defense work since striking is so satisfying. But remember the Sugar Ray Leonard quote, "Fighters get hit, good fighters don't get hit as much." Let's find out how to put ourselves into that good fighter ratio.

First let's discuss ranges in a fight. There are many concepts bandied about. One states that there are four ranges in a fight. Another says five. Yet another

Simplify! Two fight ranges: Inside and outside or simply fighting and not fighting.

says six. I've even heard one theory claim as many as ten(!) ranges. In theory, these demarcations allow you to select arsenal tools for the appropriate range. That's hogwash.

Let's simplify things and get to the truth of the matter. There are only two ranges in a fight. These ranges can be labeled inside and outside, or fighting and not-fighting. That's it. This bare-bones two ranges concept should make sense to NHB participants or enthusiasts because the battleground between squaring-off and the first shot are so malleable (not to mention chaotic) that any conversation trying to delineate ranges otherwise is a waste of time and not grounded in reality.

Keeping to the two ranges theory, simplifies your thoughts for a hectic game. Either the fight is on or it isn't. We can dance around the edges of striking range, but that is nothing more than choosing not to be in fighting range at a particular moment. Leave the theories and conceptual postulates to others. NHB is a sport and science of results grounded in reality.

14 Straight boxing defense

Defensive work in boxing is a science unto itself and deserves more consideration and pages than found here. For an expanded look at boxing defense theory, see any of the boxing titles by this publisher including *Boxing Mastery: Advanced Technique, Tactics and Strategies from the Sweet Science* by yours truly.

What I have provided are the "gotta haves" — the roots of a solid stonewall defense that can be learned quickly and works against a high-line kicking arsenal as well.

This stonewall defense does not provide individual defensive techniques for each offensive strike described. Such an endeavor would be futile. A solid stonewall defense does not mean that you have to identify the incoming weapon (such as jab, cross elbow, high kick, ax or hammer) and then choose a corresponding tool. This would be folly since the stress of incoming strikes and oxygen deficiency incurred in the midst of a match make fine distinctions in making these identifications impossible and useless.

Ready position
From here simple, short movements are made to block all incoming salvos — the essence of the stonewall defense.

Instead, you will be defending against angle of attack. For example, the defense described for a low hook to the body is the same defense for a round kick delivered to the same target. There is no reason to differentiate responses to attack angles. To do so merely creates confusion and slows the fighter's progress appreciably.

With this in mind, once you've read through the defensive arsenal and realize you have not found a defense for a specific strike, check the arsenal for a defensive tool that defends the angle of concern. Just plug that tool into the scheme of the fight. It's that easy.

Stonewall defense

Jab catch Right cover Left cover

Right body cover Left body cover

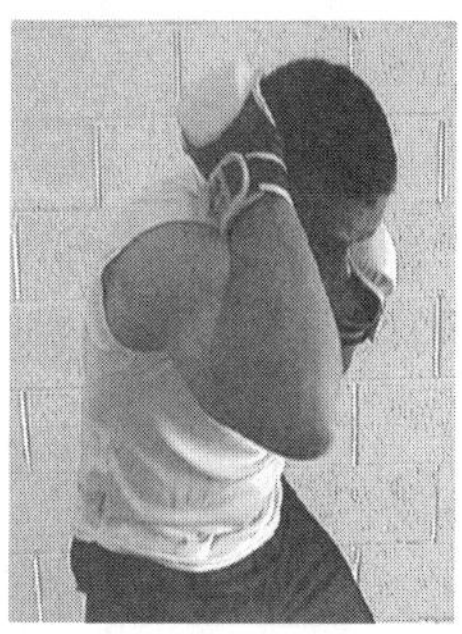

Overhand cover

Stonewall defense in profile

Ready position

Upper body defenses

Lower body defenses

Jab catch

- To defend the jab, move your rear hand from its position on your cheek.
- Bring it approximately 8-10 inches in front of your face with the palm facing out.
- Receive the punch in the palm of your hand.
- Smack the punch so that the fist doesn't take your hand and drive it into your face.
- Resist the urge to pat the jab at a downward or inside angle. This brings your defending hand away from your face leaving you open.
- Return your hand to guard position.

Cross cover

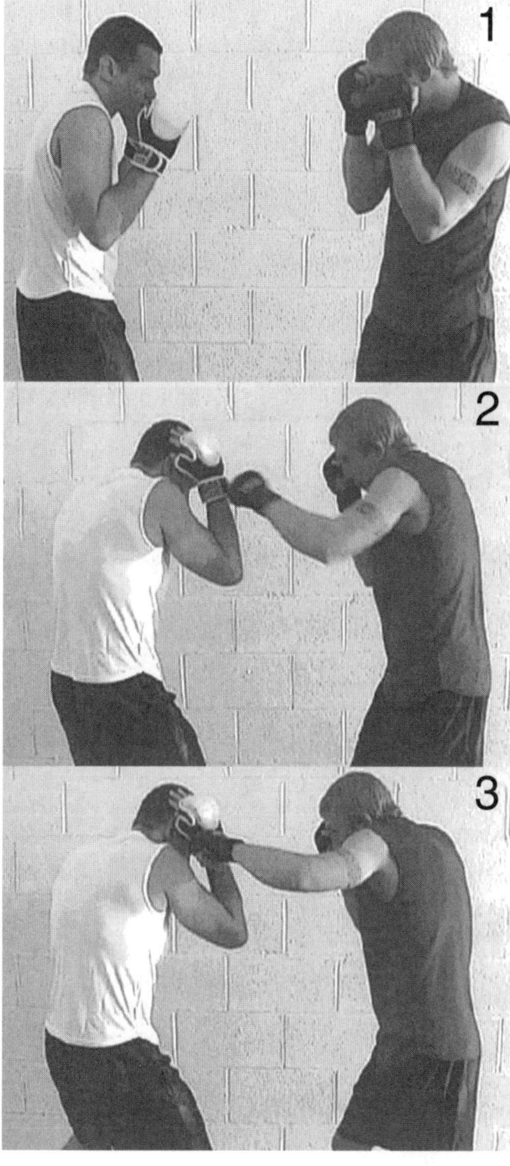

- As the cross is fired, bring your lead hand toward your lead ear.

- Open your hand and cover your ear with your hand. It is important that only your fingertips make contact with the skull. Using the palm provides very little shock absorption and can allow the suction of your palm to ring your ear.

- Dip your stance as you receive the punch.

- Return to position.

Hook cover

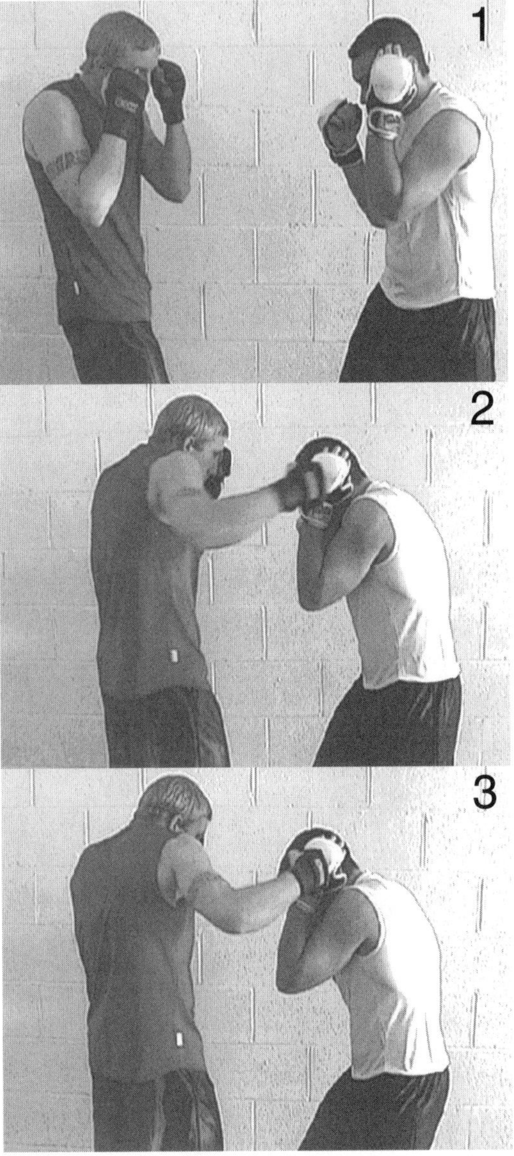

- Cover in the same manner as the cross cover, but when you dip your stance, lean into your opponent slightly to cut angle off the hook.

- This technique is performed against both lead and rear hooks.

Uppercut cover

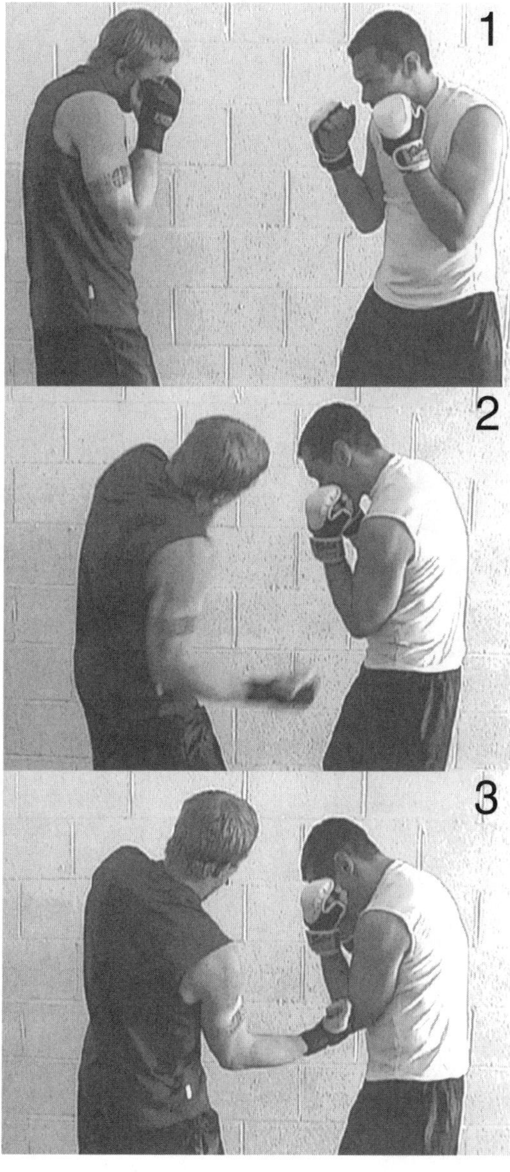

- This is similar to the hook covering motion.
- Here, as the uppercut is traveling toward you, turn the mirror side of the body toward the punch. Turn your right toward his left uppercut and vice versa.
- Pull your elbows in tight to your body and receive the punch on the forearm(s).

Overhand cover

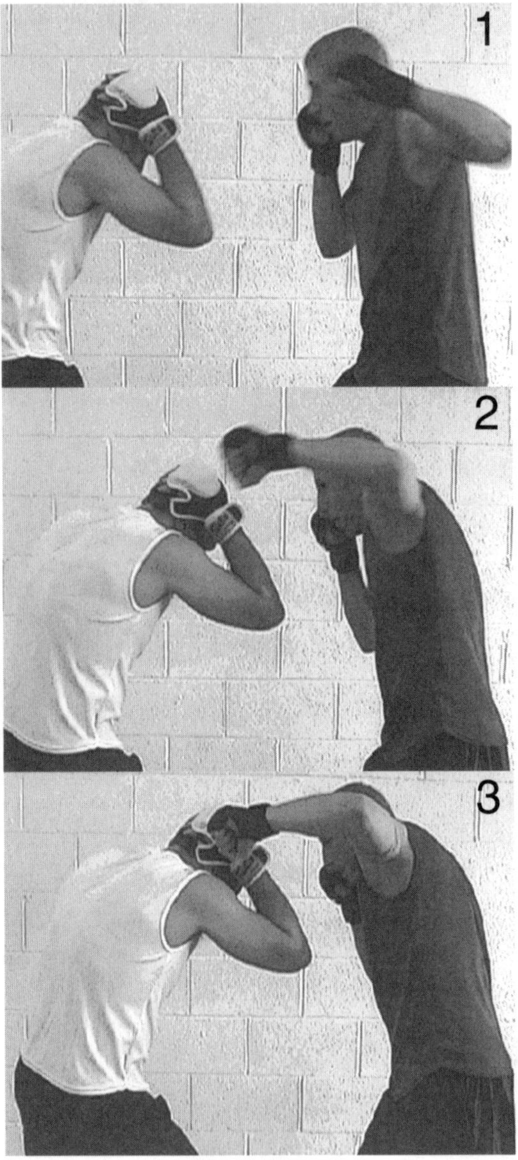

● Again using the hook cover, drape your fingers over the back of your head and allow your inner wrist to cover your ear to guard against the eccentric angle.

Defending body shots

● Using the stonewall concept to defend body shots is easier than defending head shots. Again, keep in mind that the defensive arsenal can be greatly expanded, but this stonewall concept serves its purposes in both efficiency and effectiveness.

Defending straight body shots

● Remember, we are defending angle of attack — not specific technique — so this defense can be used for strikes like low jabs, crosses and jab kicks.

● As the strike is launched, direct one or both elbows in front of the target and dip your stance to absorb the shock. It is wise to dip your stance on all stonewall defenses because the legs are natural shock absorbers. Dipping 6-8 inches can go a long way toward mitigating impact.

Defending body shots

Defending hooking body shots
Adjust your arm on the side that is attacked so that the blow will be absorbed by the arm and not by any other portion of your body.

Be sure to receive the blow on both gates of the arm (upper and forearm) simultaneously. Receiving the impact on only one portion can create cumulative damage slowing your attack speed.

Defending body uppercuts
These shots are defended in the same manner as the high angle uppercut.

15
Elbow defenses

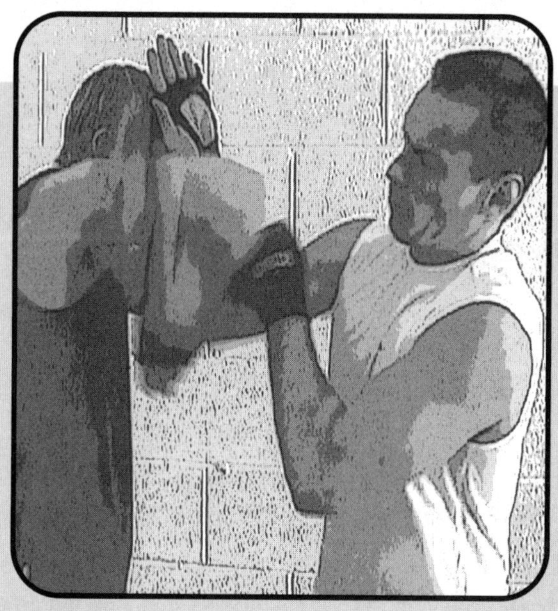

Recall the peculiar rear hand position described when throwing your own elbow and you will have the root of the defense for the elbow. The hand raised high on the head with palm out is the optimum position from which to defend.

Elbow catch

- As the opponent launches his cross elbow (here his right), raise your left arm and place the back of your hand on your forehead, palm facing the opponent.

- Attempt to catch the elbow in the palm of your upraised hand; failing that, the elbow will meet the soft musculature of your inner forearm, which is far better than it biting into the bones of the forearm.

- When receiving the elbow, smack into it to mitigate some of its force.

- This smack also creates a downward slope of your forearm that diminishes more power from the strike.

Elbow catch drill: One throws and one defends

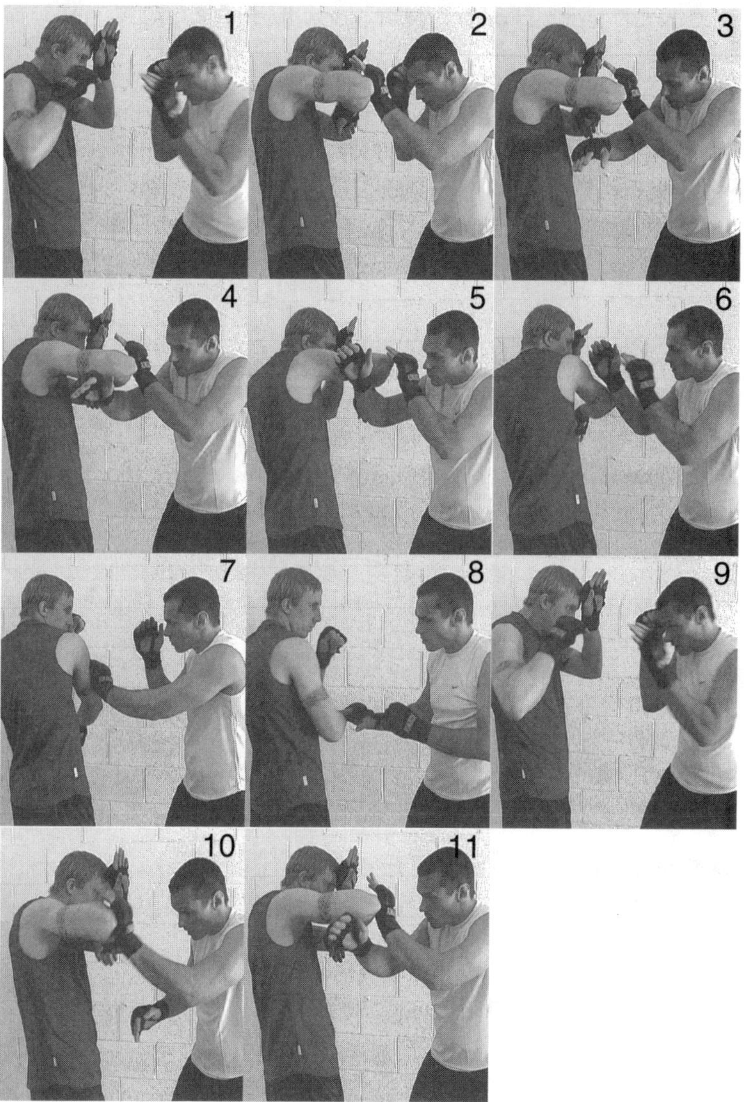

Elbow catch drill: Both throw and defend

● This drill teaches both proper elbow firing and proper elbow defense.

● Once you understand the rhythm, continue the cycles non-stop on one side for several rounds and then repeat on the other side.

● To execute, you and a training partner stand in close-quarters position.

● Your partner fires a right cross elbow in proper form.

● You receive the elbow in the palm of your left hand.

● Dip the back of your right hand behind his elbow and brush it toward the right side of your body.

● As the tip of his elbow passes, pat the back of his elbow with the palm of your left hand. This serves as a check against his returning a back elbow.

● Now fire your own right cross elbow with proper form.

● Your partner will then execute the same catch, brush, pat, return motion to bring the volley back to you.

● This drill is easier done than described. Grab a partner and work through the steps. You will have it down in no time.

● This artificial construct will not occur in a fight, but the catch and other individual aspects can and do. I highly recommend this drill.

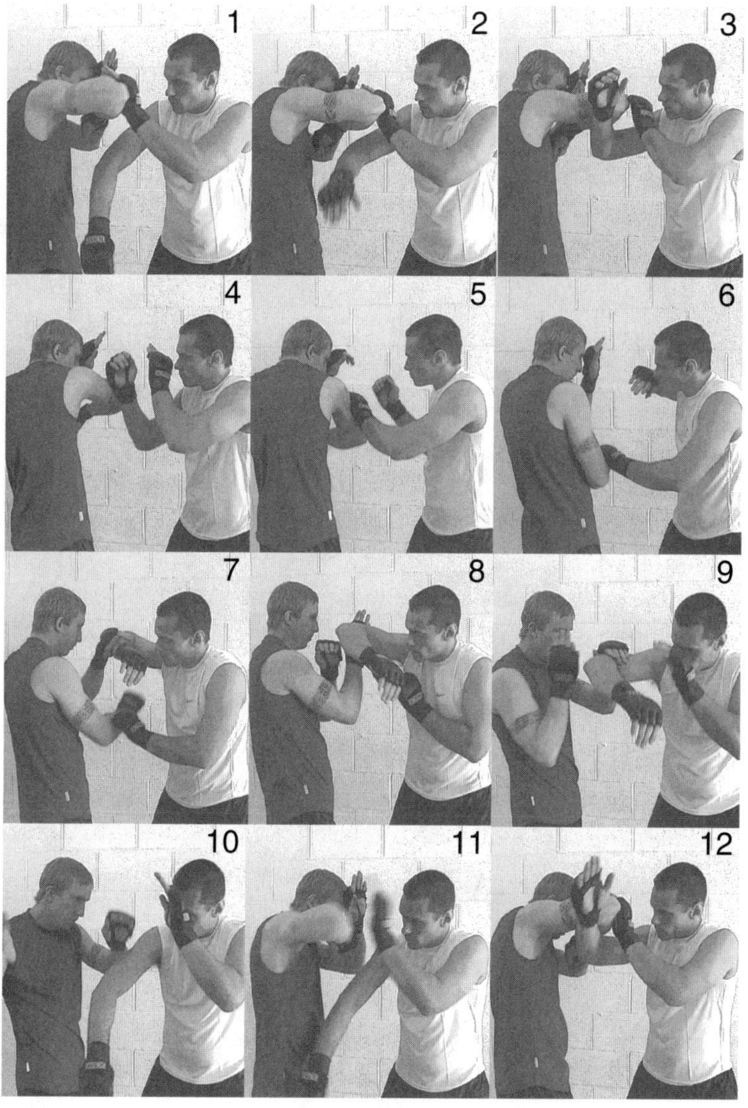
1
2
3
4
5
6
7
8
9
10
11
12

Elbow lift

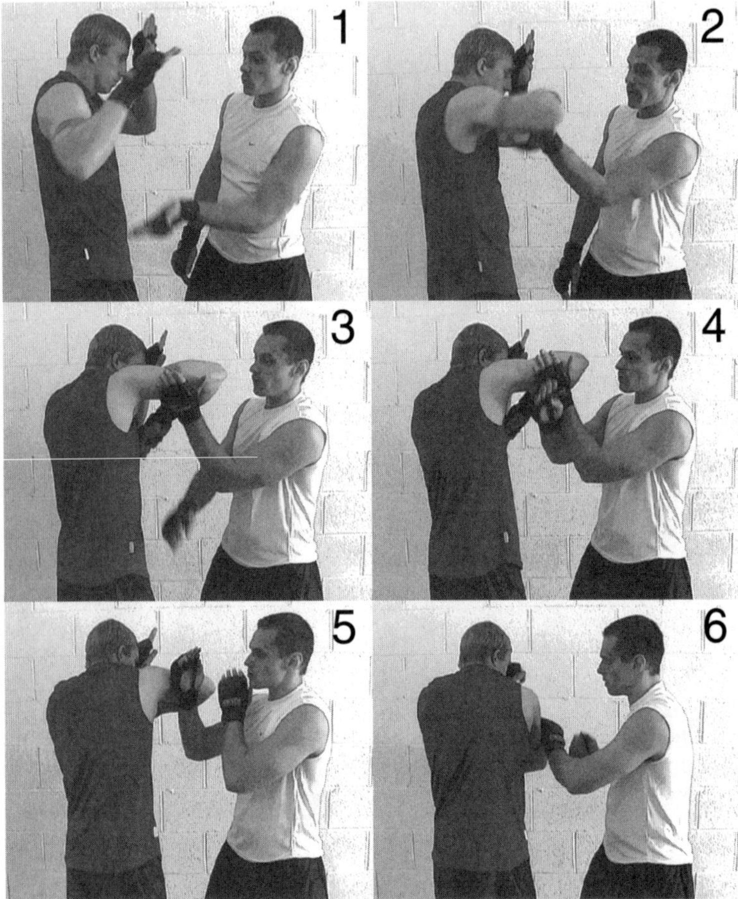

- The elbow catch is the optimum defense because it works from good defense position.
- Sometimes, though, you are not in good position when an elbow is fired and you need a "Hail Mary" play. That's the elbow lift.
- The opponent fires a right cross elbow and your left hand is below catch position.
- Use the palm of your left hand to slap the incoming elbow up directing it away from you.

Elbow lift drill: Both throw and defend

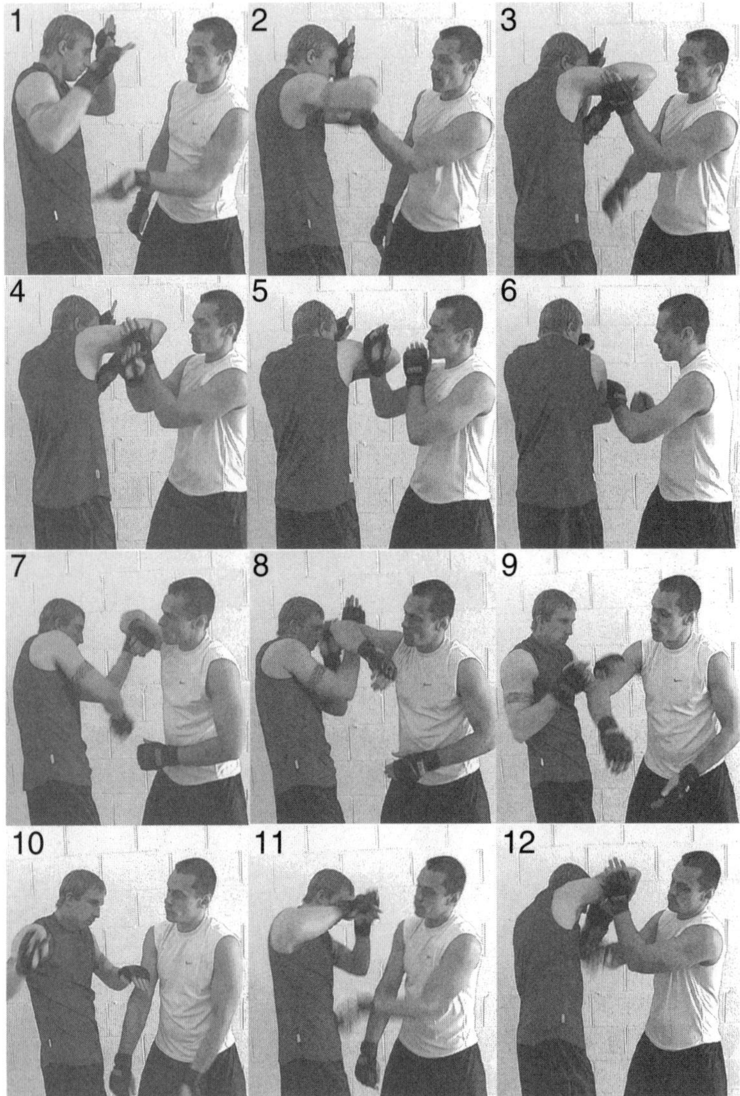

● Here's a cyclical drill for the lift.

● Your partner fires a right cross elbow.

● You lift it with your left palm.

● When you lift, use your right hand to brush as in the catch drill. Pat in the same manner described before and return a right elbow for your partner to execute the same lift technique.

● Continue for several rounds and work both sides.

Catch and lift blender drill

- With some imagination, you can blend these drills.

- Switch attack sides (right elbow attack to left elbow attack and vice versa) simply by pulling the attacking elbow back in a long windup to signal the switch. Be sure you telegraph while drilling — you do not want to be hit with an elbow.

- Switch from catching to lifting, as you see fit, with no need to signal your partner since the change does not affect his portion of the drill.

- You can also test each other's pat portion of the drill by occasionally slipping a back elbow into the mix as your cross elbow is being patted out of position.

- Working these elbow defense drills diligently will better prepare you to throw and defend them reflexively.

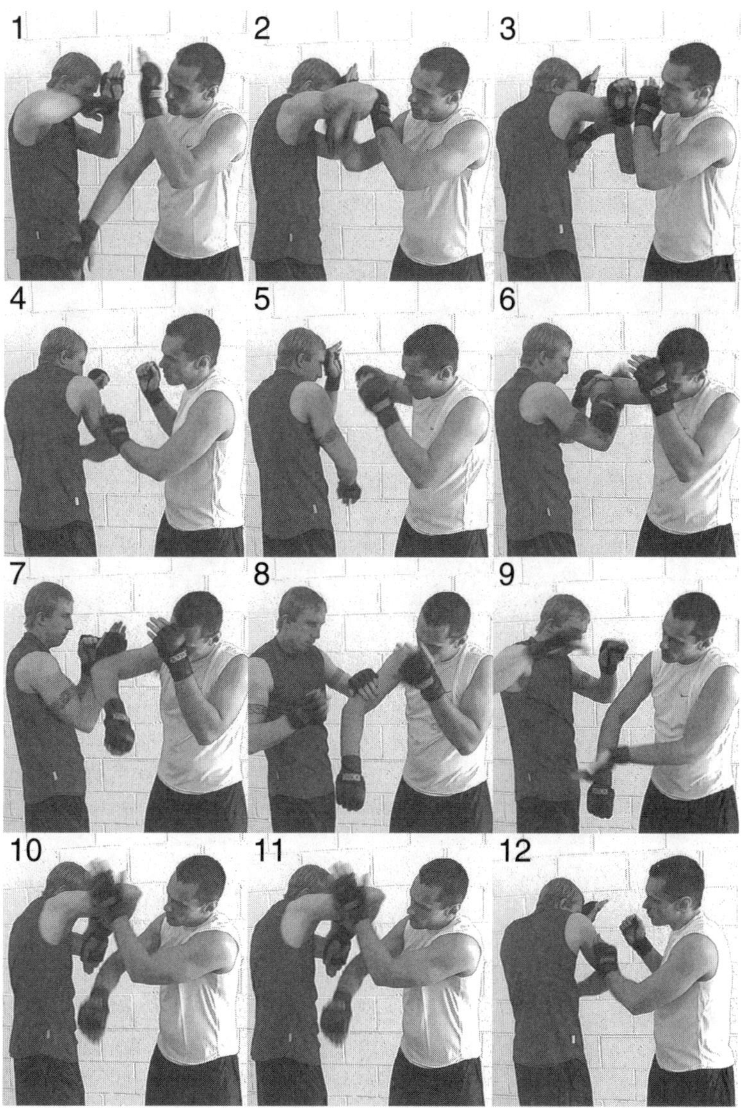

Starting with elbow catching and going into elbow lifting ...

More blend drill

.. switching sides and elbowing catching ...

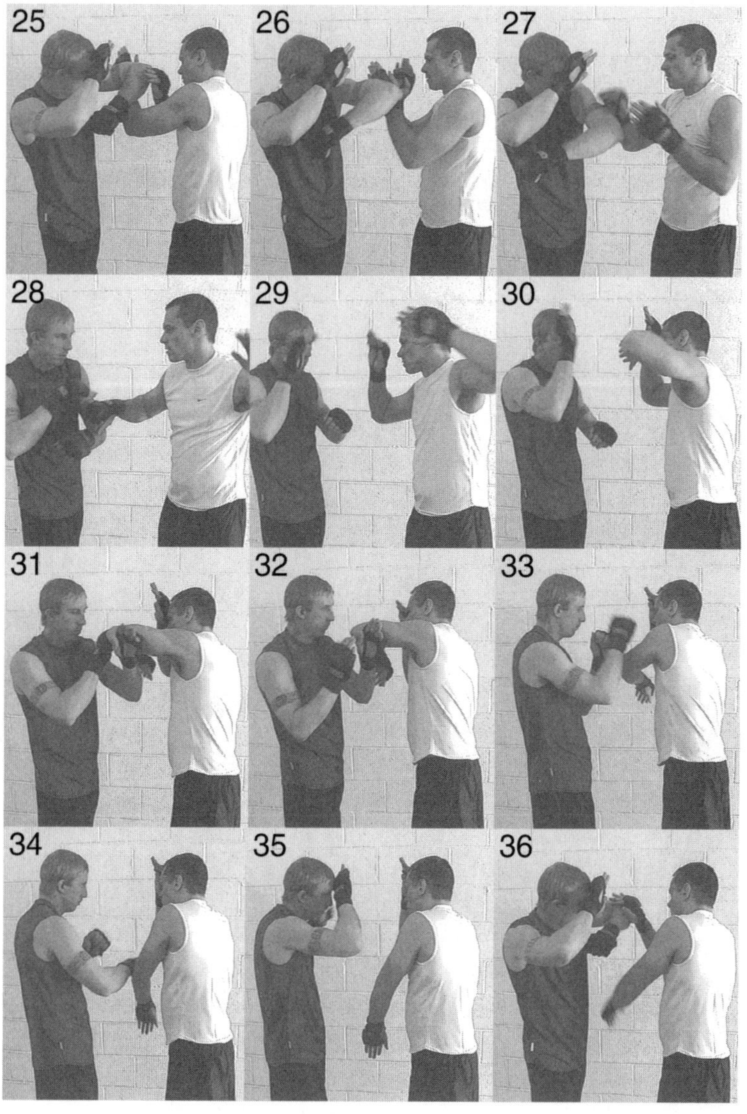
25
26
27
28
29
30
31
32
33
34
35
36

16
Head butt defense

Head butts are damaging weapons, but fortunately are fairly easy to counter. Beyond staying aware of an opponent's head when inside a clinch, these two defensive methods should go a long way to steer you clear of these shots.

Cup

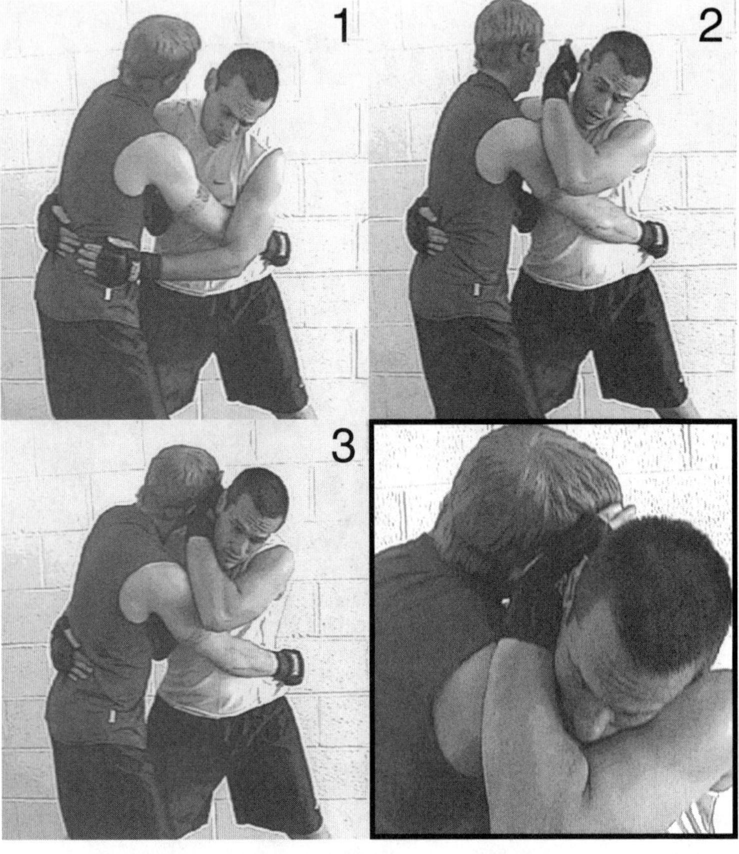

● Simply place the palm of your hand on an opponent's head to muffle his head-butt attack.

● The cup is most useful as a preemptive defense inside a clinch where you can leave a hand in the cup position to prevent clinch head butts.

Jam

- A simple but effective tool for stopping cold any free head butt and many clinch head butts.

- As your opponent launches the head butt, shove the palm of either or both hands into his head or shoulder(s).

- This movement effectively stops his momentum.

17 Knee defense

Knees are formidable high-percentage weapons, so you need a good arsenal to counter these awesome tools. Defenses for noncohesive knees (knees without a clinch) and knees fired inside two varieties of clinches follow.

Spike

● An opponent fires a straight knee.

● Drop your hips back, dip your stance and aim the point of your lead elbow into the top of his attacking thigh.

Pat out

● When an opponent fires his straight knee, use your hand to pat his knee to the outside (away from his chest or midline). The pat is a small motion of your arm requiring that you use only your palm against the inside of his knee.

● Because your opponent will be unstable standing on one leg, he will step widely to his outside making your opportunities for follow-up rather tasty.

Pat in

- The flip side of a pat out.

- Pat his knee toward his midline to yield the same results.

- Pats can be executed with either the lead or rear hands and to the outside or inside.

Jam

- Just as you can jam the head butt, you can jam a straight knee.
- If you are in tight, strike his shoulder or head sharply with the palm of either or both hands to stop the momentum and take his base.
- In all knee counters, I advise you to exploit an opponent's single-leg base. As soon as you counter his knee, counter strike with crisp combination work before he can fully recover his balance.

Proper over-under clinch

● Many knees have been fired from this particular position, both straight knees and round knees, even round knees to the head.

● That's a shame, for if you root the over-under properly, the possibility of executing knees drops to zero.

● Here we describe how to root the over-under clinch so that when an opponent throws a knee, a small jerk of the clinch can pull him off base. Your clinch remains intact because your hands are not needed to defend against the knee.

● The key is not to lean into your opponent. Instead, root down. Leaning in puts no weight on an opponent making his knee attack an easy proposition. Rooting down changes that.

● Foot position matters. You will always have your overhook-side leg forward. If you are overhooking with your left arm (see photo) you will have the left leg forward. This makes sense when you realize that you are rooting down, and you must put the majority of your weight on top of his underhook arm, which is on your overhook side. It is a physical impossibility to place weight on your underhook, you would collapse to the mat.

● That's all there is to it. Root this clinch properly to remove the knee threat.

● I recommend pummeling (switching sides) from this position while paying close attention to foot position and the rooting angle to make this second nature.

● We will not delve into the technicalities of clinch work because the subject needs its own text.

Right way

Wrong ways

With overhooking leg forward (top) an opponent cannot attack with his knee. Otherwise he can (right).

Head rest

- An opponent is seeking an optimum clinch as described in the offensive arsenal section.

- The many ways to snake and resnake this clinch are mainly for straight striking contests where the give and take of knees is uninterrupted by the possibility of a body lock or other takedown attempt.

- The head rest defense gives you head control and allows you to root an opponent's base down like the over-under clinch removing much of the knee threat.

- To execute, snake your forearm (here the left forearm) over the top of both of his arms as he grabs you behind the head.

- Fit your forearm snugly into the crook of his arms and press your forehead tightly into the top of your forearm.

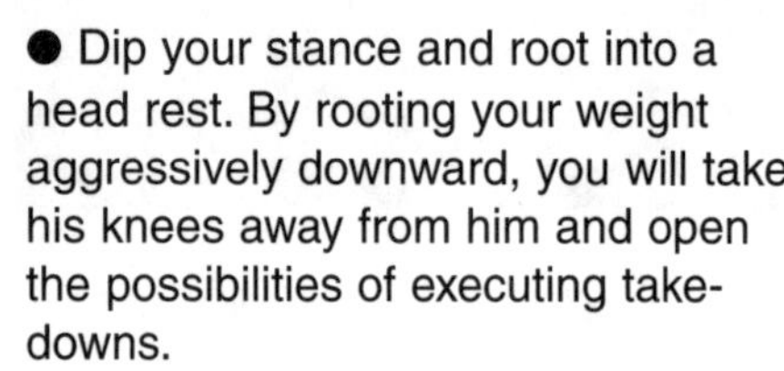

- Dip your stance and root into a head rest. By rooting your weight aggressively downward, you will take his knees away from him and open the possibilities of executing take-downs.

- I heartily encourage you to work this technique and play with the possibilities.

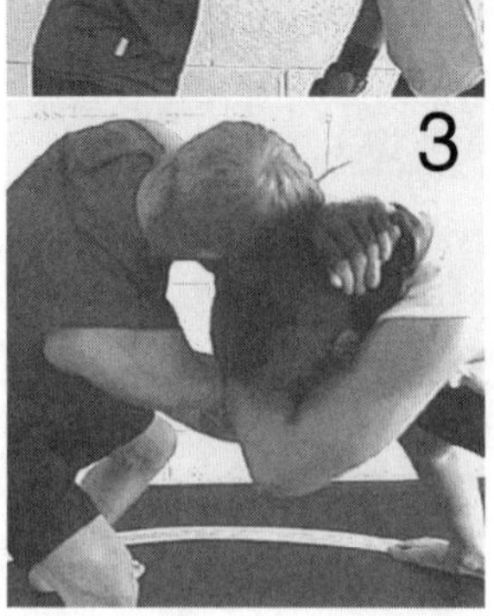

1
2
3
4

18
Kick defense

Much of kicking defense is pulled from the straight boxing stonewall defense. The only difference is you will have to be even more scrupulous about using the legs as shock absorbers to take the bite out of these strong weapons.

High round stonewall

● Against a head kick, execute the same stonewall as for a high hook punch.

Medium round stonewall

- Against body kicks, execute the same stonewall defense as for the body hooks.

- Remember to use both gates of the arm and not merely your forearm.

Low round point

- We have no previous stonewall example to fall back on versus the thigh kick. I do not advocate the simple lifting and shielding with the shin because this "defense" is somewhat painful.

- If you are already acclimated to this defense, continue to use it since you have already paid dues in regards to shin acclimatization. I used this method myself for years before switching to the following method.

- For those looking for a defense that will make an opponent think twice about throwing a thigh kick, the point defense is for you.

- As the kick approaches, raise the targeted leg and point the knee at the incoming kick.

- You are not striking the kick with your knee but "allowing" the opponent to kick into your knee point.

- Do not worry if your accuracy is off, the raised knee position still protects and deflects the force of the kick even if you were unable to score a direct hit with the point.

Purring point

- The knee point can also be used to counter purring kicks.
- Point the tip of your knee high on your opponent's shin to take much of the steam out of his purring attack.

High straight kick stonewall

- Against a high straight kick to your head, merely close the parallel shells of your forearms to deflect the attack.

- Rock back with the body to help absorb the blow.

Medium straight kick stonewall

- Here an opponent fires a straight kick at your body.
- Close the forearm shells and sink your hips back upon impact to mitigate the blow.

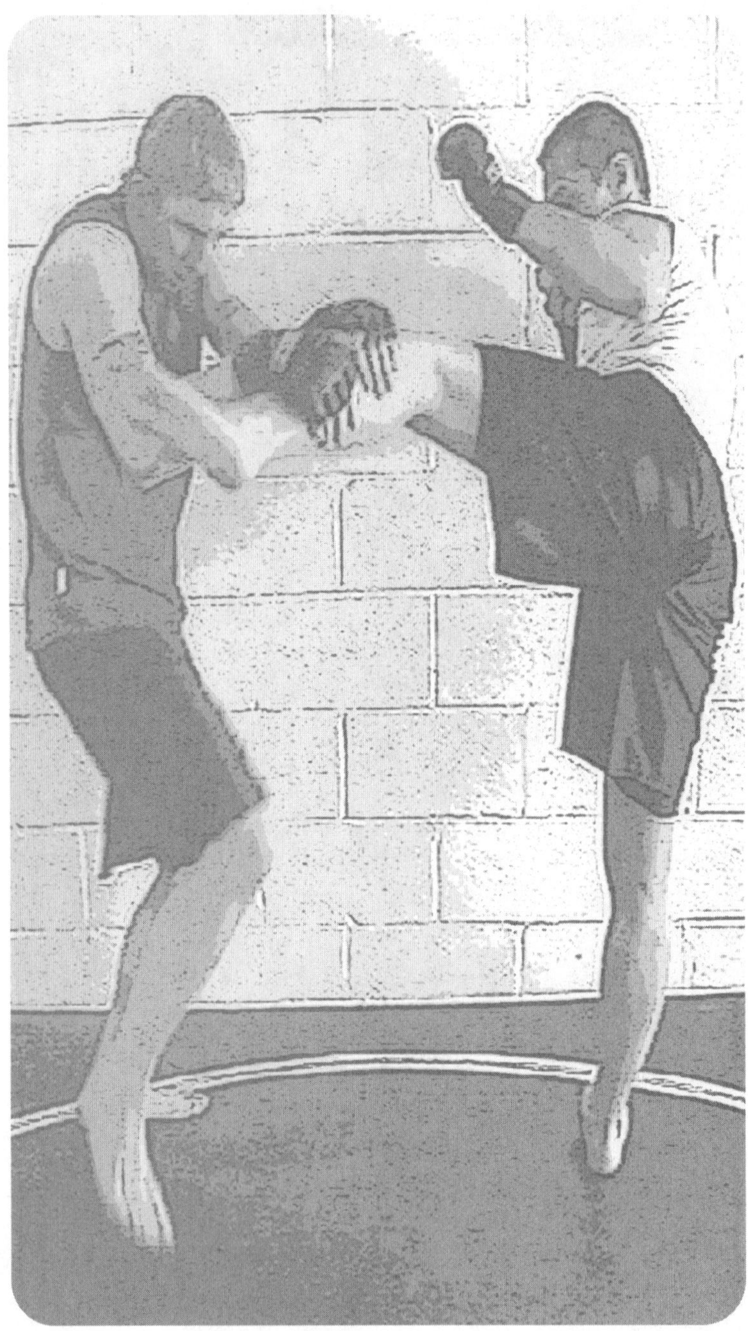

19 Pick offs

You already have a solid defense for practically every aspect of the striking game. Now, let's take a look how to turn portions of that defense into damaging weapons. This strategy is known as pick offs. You've already encountered the root of this idea in the knee point defense against thigh kicks. Pick offs are merely designated defenses that direct the points of elbows or knees into an incoming weapon. They have the benefits of being defenses and pain-inflictors. Pick offs will not end fights, but are nice tools to throw into the mix making an opponent's job all the more painful.

Punch pick offs

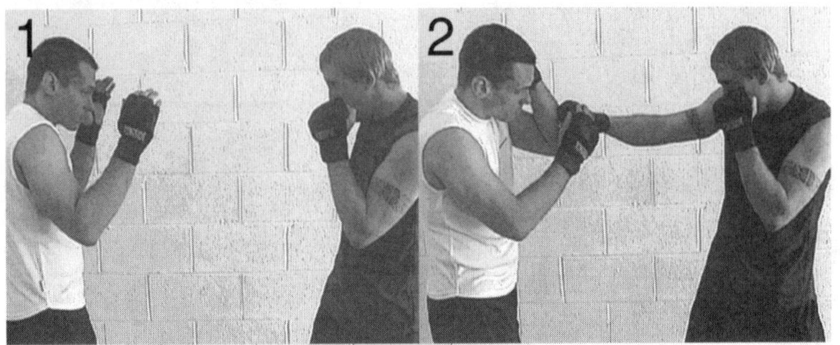

- Punch pick offs can be used only against straight shots.
- The object is to deliver the point of the elbow directly into your opponent's incoming fist.
- You are not striking the fist, you are merely placing your elbow in the path of his attack and letting his force do the damage.

Lead to rear guidance

- Guide the punch with your lead hand into the point of your rear elbow.

Rear to lead guidance

- Allow the rear hand to guide the punch into the lead elbow.

Skeet shooting

● Using no guidance hand, merely point the elbows into the paths of incoming punches.

Punch pick off fail-safe

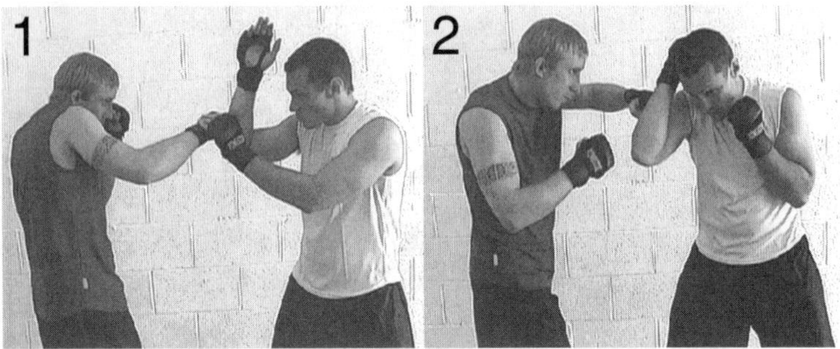

● It is important to keep your forearms in a vertical plane when executing pick offs. You can very well miss a pick off and the vertical plane acts as your fail-safe. The horizontal elbow does not allow for this backup.

High round kick pick off

● Still using the stonewall strategy with a small adjustment, use one hand to guide the incoming head kick to your other elbow.

● You can execute this technique for lead hand guide to rear elbow and rear hand guide to lead elbow.

Mid round kick pick off

● Use the same strategy, techniques and limb combinations as in the high-line round pick offs.

Knee drags

● This is a pick off strategy that can be used for either the high or mid-level round kicks.

● I suggest becoming adept at the standard pick offs before moving to knee drags.

● The knee drag is executed by using the twin shields of your forearms (inner forearms facing your opponent's incoming shin).

● Upon impact, immediately use your forearms/hands to drag/slap the kick down.

● As the kicking limb is slapped down, execute an up-knee into the slapped limb.

● The knee drag is executed on the side of attack. For example, a kick delivered to the left side of your body will receive a left knee and vice versa.

● The knee drag can be performed on each side of the body and for both the head and body kicks.

Knee drag with pick off

● It can also be used in tandem with the previous kick pick offs — lead hand guide to rear elbow to knee drag or rear hand guide to lead elbow to knee drag.

● Remember, pick offs should be added to your defensive tools, not used in place of them. Be sure that your stonewall is firm and reflexive before adding the pick off extras. Each and every tool in your defensive arsenal should be drilled in isolation rounds and then in combination to ensure fluidity of movement.

20
Ground 'n' pound

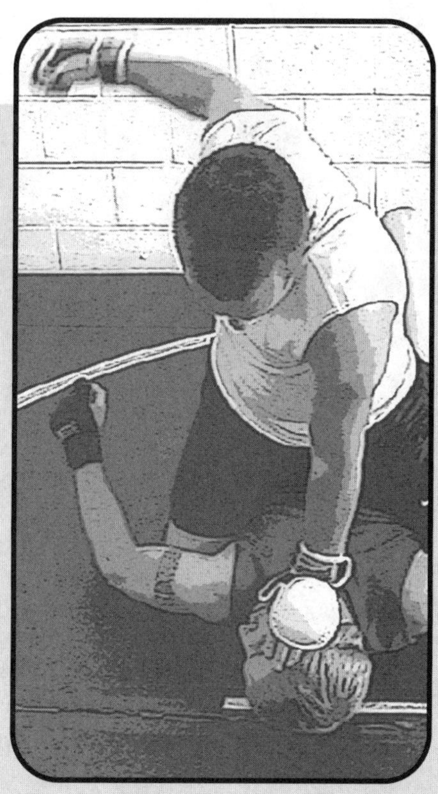

Since the game is NHB, chances are the fight will wind up on the ground at some point. When it does there is no need to abandon your striking game.

We will take a look at tools that transfer to the ground easily, a few that need some adjustments and a few ways to limit or at least mitigate the effectiveness of strikes if you are on the receiving end.

Mounted / top saddle punching

- This is a great position to punch from, but not all fighters use it effectively. Once mounted, many fighters sit up high and go to work with both hands planning to use the punches as a setup for the choke. That is, the opponent turns his back to hide from the strikes so that a choke can be applied. That's fine against an unskilled, outclassed, or gassed-out opponent, but against today's quick-to-get-up fighters, you may be headed for a lost position. So let's look at punching from the top saddle as an opportunity to finish.

- Instead of sitting up high and firing both hands, post the palm of one hand on your opponent's face and force it to the mat.

- Post all of your weight through his face and punch with the other hand.

- This will lead to either better strike damage or a tighter submission setup (right).

- An abbreviated arsenal that can be used from all top positions follows.

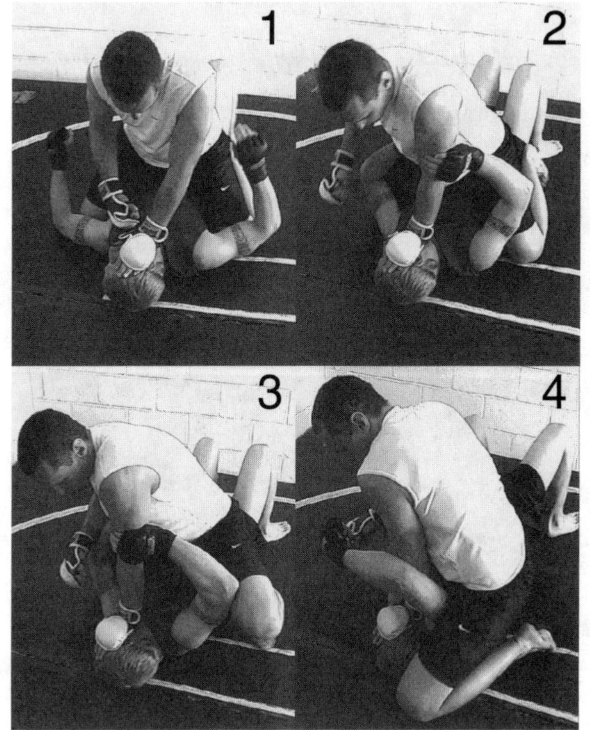
1
2
3
4

Hammer

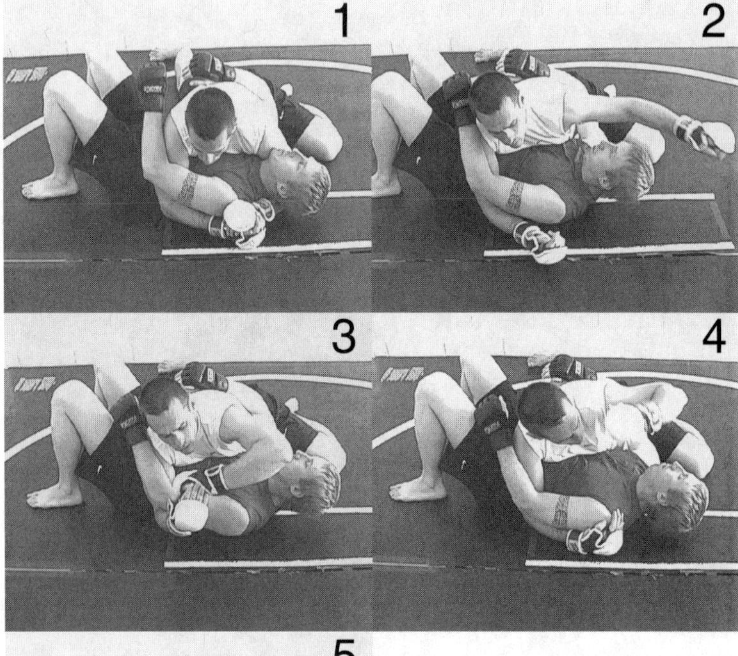

- Hammers are ideal for the ground 'n' pound strategy because they:
- Carry more force than standard punching.
- Can be fired in the tight confines of the ground game.
- Allow you to strike hard without damaging your hands.
- Can be fired from awkward positions.
- Can be fired at the head or any soft portion of the torso for maximum effect.

More hammering

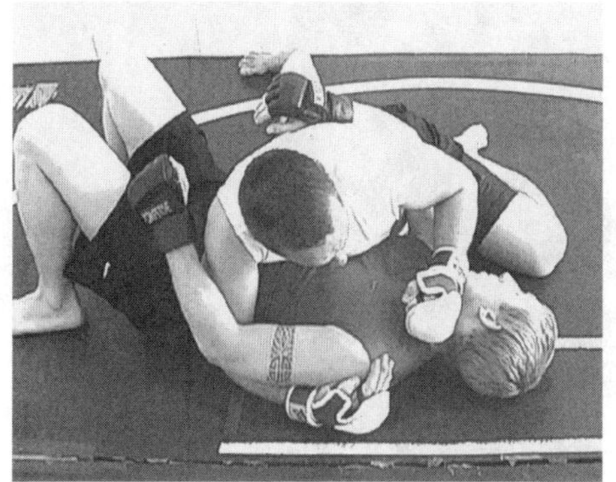

Cram

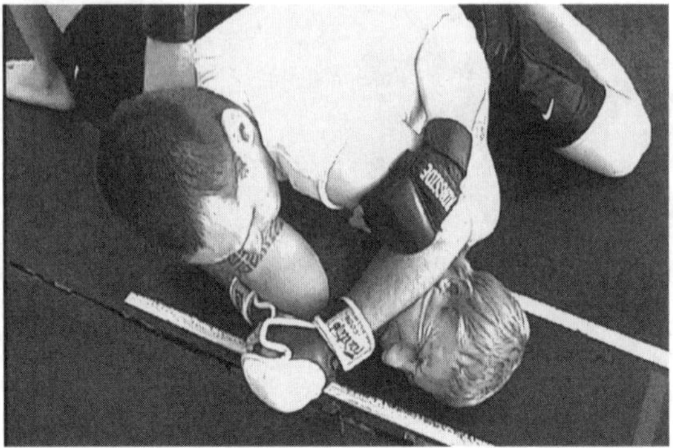

- The cram is a great weapon to make an opponent uncomfortable or to set up other strikes.
- It is best to cram the face or throat.

Hacksaw

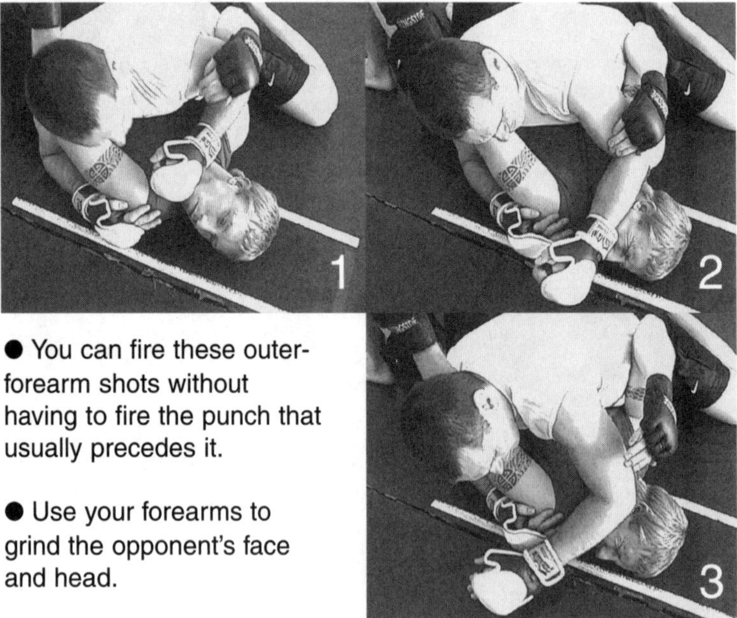

- You can fire these outer-forearm shots without having to fire the punch that usually precedes it.

- Use your forearms to grind the opponent's face and head.

Elbows

- Elbow strikes are illegal in most events, but for a complete arsenal, be aware how these are best fired.
- Use cross and down elbows when mounted on an opponent.
- Use back elbows when cross-body on an opponent.
- You can use the elbows also to dig or "jones" into an opponent to create movement for setups or to keep him on the defensive.
- Dig targets are the face, throat, sternum and soft torso tissue.

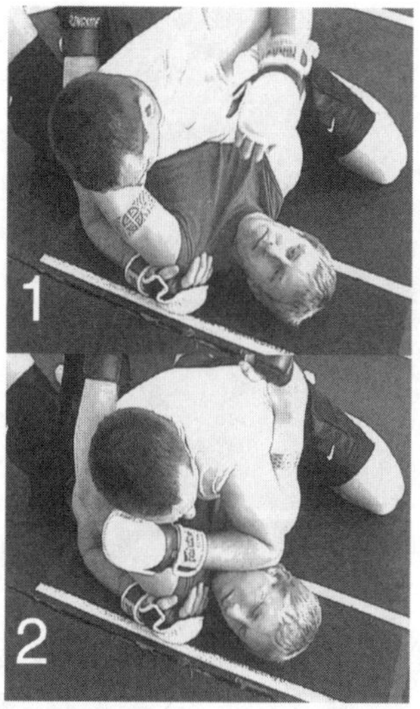

Cross elbow

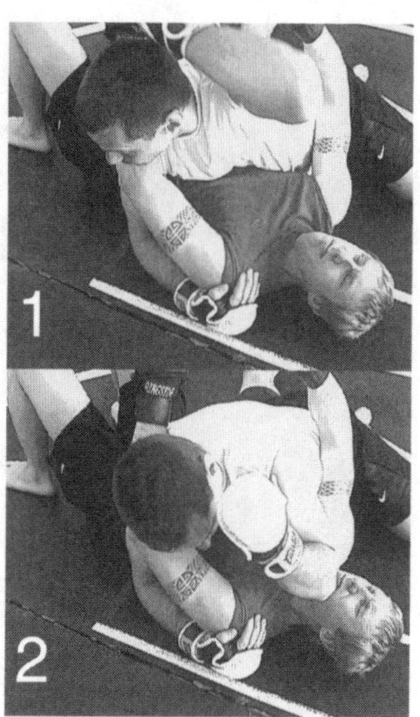

Down elbow

More elbow work

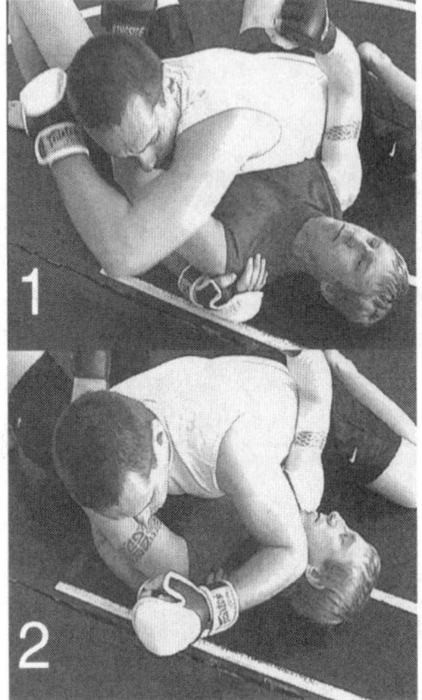

Back elbow

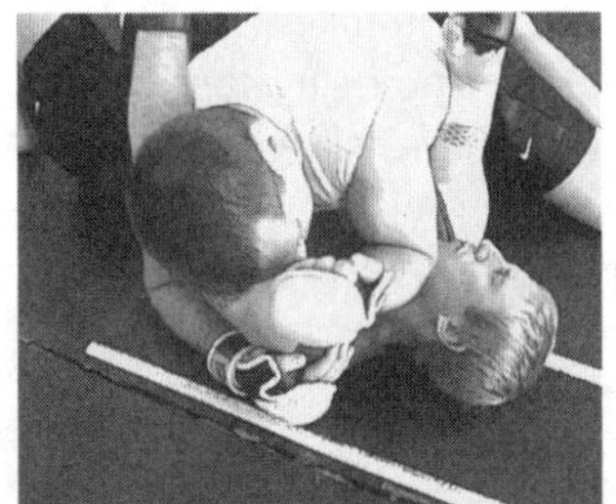

Elbow digs

Shoulder jam

● You can use a shoulder as a cram when in a top position.

● Fire it into the face or underneath the chin.

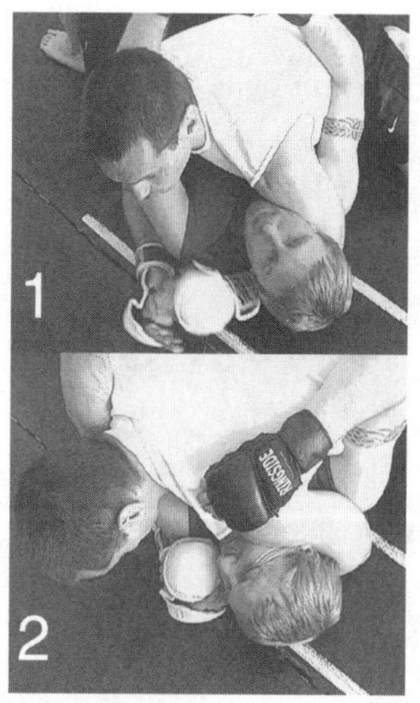
Shoulder jam

Head jam

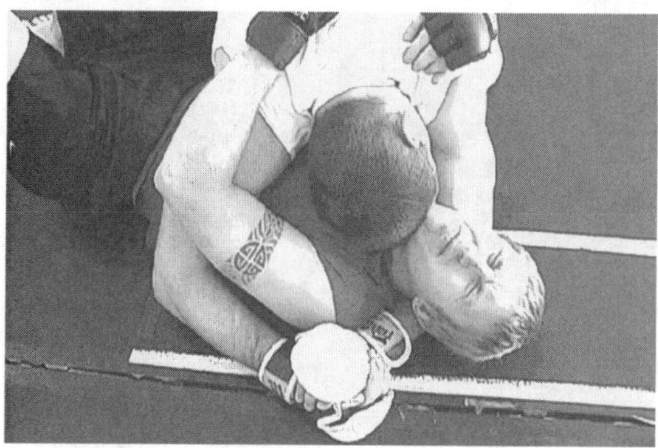

● Head butts are illegal in most events (as they should be). I don't recommend them in a self-defense context because they are difficult to fire on the ground without risking a cut.

● The head can be used like the cram and shoulder jam by applying pressure to the face or under an opponent's chin.

Drop knee

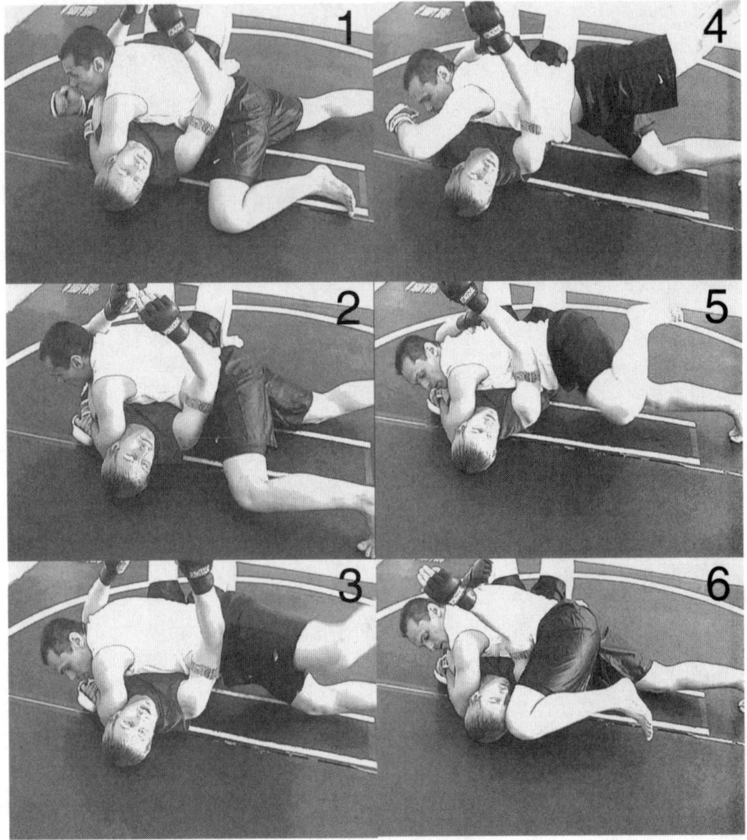

- An excellent tool from the cross-body or top-body/lateral-press position.
- To fire, keep your chest pressure tight into an opponent to stabilize him.
- Elevate your hips momentarily. Be sure not to put your weight on the mat while doing so — leave the weight on your opponent.
- Cock either knee to the sky and drop it into your opponent.
- The best targets are the torso and the head.

Heel chop

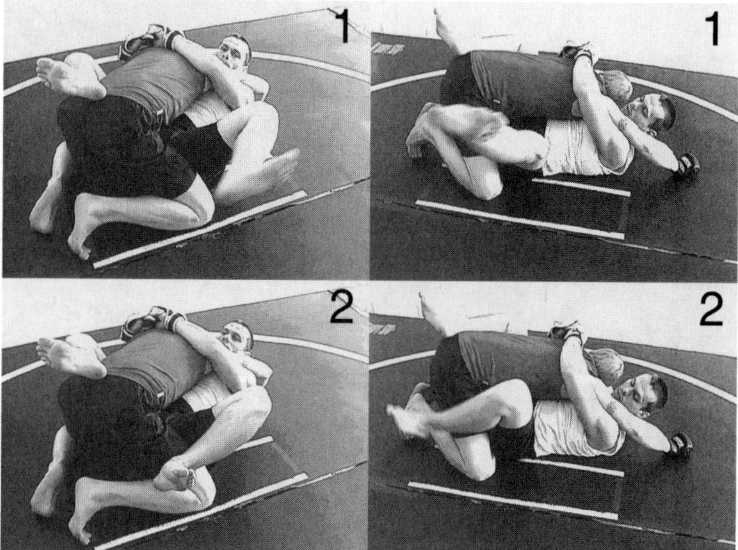

- When fighting off your back, you have many strikes available to you if the opponent has you grounded (he is standing and you are on the mat). That is a separate subject from ground 'n' pound. (See Resources for grounded material.)

- The primary strike for the guard player is the heel chop. Elbow strikes and punching from the back carry little mass and won't submit or turn an opponent over, which is the main concern in this position.

- Heel chops are not executed to an opponent's back. This causes little damage and the angle dictates you are primarily striking with soft calf musculature.

- Instead, use short heel chops to your opponent's thighs and calves when he sits inside your legs. This is a much better tool to inspire his relocation.

Lock defense

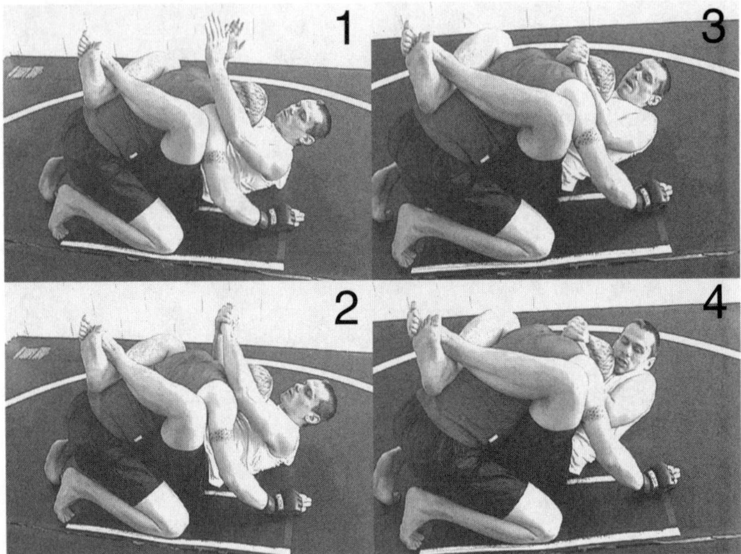

- When caught on your back, your first priority is to escape and get back in the game. If your initial escape attempt is unsuccessful, use the lock.
- The lock is a head control tactic that allows you to keep the opponent tight to you making him less likely to strike and takes more wallop out of the strikes he does throw.
- The lock also can lead to many submission setups, which we do not cover in this volume.
- Starting from the guard/bottom scissors position, wrap one hand around the back of your opponent's neck placing the inner wrist against his neck.
- Grip your hands palm-to-palm while keeping the inner wrist position on your opponent's neck.
- Grind your inner wrist through the back of his neck while arching your chest through his face to keep him tight. This will change his game plan.

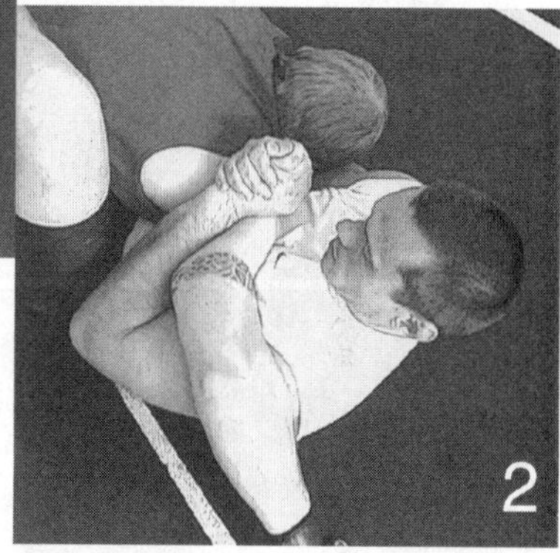

● You also can execute the lock against the back of his shoulder if his head is not initially available. Observe the same rules to reap the maximum benefits from this deceptive strategy.

● That's it for ground 'n' pound. I suggest tossing a heavy bag on the mat and working each of these tools for a few rounds and then in combinations. Remember to focus on keeping good pressure through the bag or your opponent while drilling, because you cannot strike for maximum damage unless you are in control.

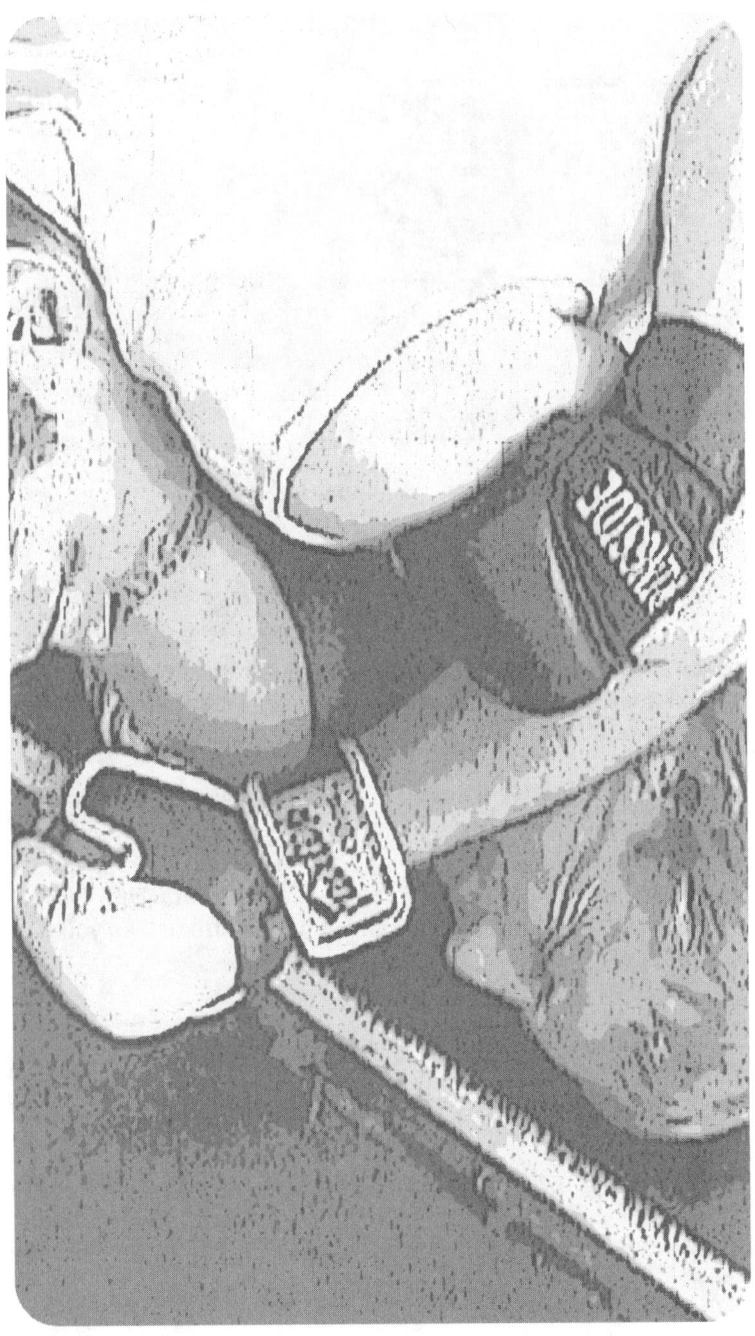

21 Combinations

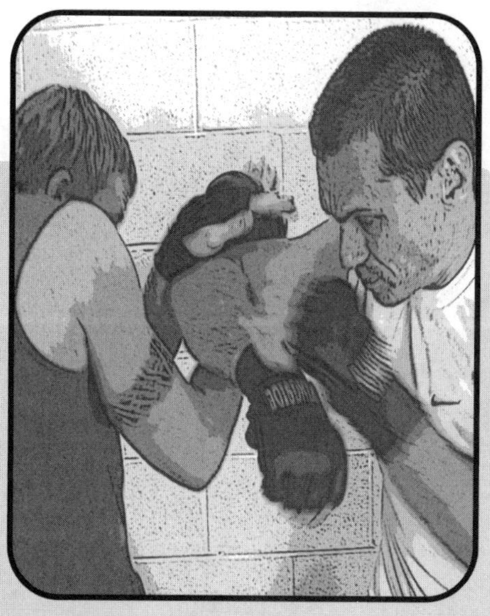

The crux of this volume is to introduce the voluminous NHB arsenal and define how it differentiates from standard boxing and kick-boxing arsenals. Fights are not won by individual techniques but by combinations. The art and science of creating combinations could push valid NHB combinations into the stratosphere.

We illustrate only a few. Straight boxing combinations are discussed in greater depth in the volumes recommended in the Resources section (see in particular *Boxing Mastery*). This is a short list of high-percentage combinations to get you going. Once you have mastered these, the creation of your own combinations should be a piece of cake.

Jab / thigh kick

Jab / straight knee

Jab / rear cross elbow

Cross / lead cross elbow

Jab / rear up elbow

Thigh kick / cross / hook

Cross / optimum clinch / knee

Jab / cross / lead up elbow

Hook / cross / hammer

Jab / rear straight knee / false clinch / head butt

Jab / cross / hook / thigh kick

Cross / hook / cross / lead hammer

Hook / cross / hook / thigh kick

Jab / cram / cross / thigh kick

Jab / cross / hook / rear cross elbow

Up elbow / rear cross elbow / optimum clinch / straight knee

Cross / lead up elbow / cross / lead cross elbow

Jab / cross / rear straight knee / lead back hammer

Rear uppercut / hook / rear uppercut / optimum clinch / straight knee

Jab / cross / straight knee / lead cross elbow

Jab / cross / hook / cross / optimum clinch / straight knee

Jab / cross / hook / thigh kick / optimum clinch / up knee / clinch breaker

Jab / cross / hook / cross / hook / rear cross elbow

Jab / cross / hook / cross / over-under clinch / purring kick / bump

22 Drilling

OK, you have all the information. How do you put it together in tight construction so that the knowledge is really yours? The answer is live drilling. We aren't striving for mindless, rote repetition but a drill hierarchy that obeys the 80/20 rule we've relied on elsewhere.

It is paramount that you learn each physical action in isolation and put it through mental rehearsal and shadow practice when you first encounter it. The drill hierarchy allows you to select the best mode of drilling for the desired purpose.

Focus pads and Thai pads

The importance of a good feeder

- For duplicating conditions of the NHB striking game, there is nothing like having a skilled focus pad feeder in front of you.
- A good feeder can duplicate any shot and feed any and all targets while firing offensive shots back at you to sharpen your defensive skills.
- A good feeder calls every opening for you and then hits the openings that aren't filled in with his verbal coaching.
- A good feeder utilizes good footwork and makes you move around the training area so you don't learn to fight standing still.
- A good feeder calls combinations interspersed with defensive responses.
- A good feeder can mix in precision striking with power shot work.
- A good feeder realizes that he must be as diligent as the fighter and be able to juke and jive and mimic what the fighter is likely to encounter in the ring.
- A good feeder makes the fighter miss occasionally and alters his rhythm so that the fighter's timing does not fall into a rut.
- That's a lot to ask of a training partner, but it is of utmost importance to your progress.

● I prefer focus mitts over Thai pads. Focus mitts are lighter in weight and allow greater and faster mobility. They help create an increasingly realistic environment for the fighter. Experiment to see what works best for you.

Shadow boxing

● The fighter utilizes a mirror or his imagination to create a live opponent. It is vital that you do not fall into the trap of mindless repetition but literally see, hear, feel an opponent and attack and respond accordingly. There is much to be said for shadow-drilling. Do not neglect it.

Heavy bag drilling

● Whether hanging or used on the floor, the heavy bag helps you develop power. You can do the same with focus mitts, but heavy bags are used when you lack a skilled feeder. It is important to create the same alive attitude with the heavy bag that you strive for with the other two drilling methods. Do not fall into the rut of standing in front of the bag impressing yourself with how much you can make it swing. Incidentally, swinging the bag is a sign of improper technique. You are seeking to dent or fold the bag. That's power.

There you have it — an entire book of high-percentage NHB offensive and defensive weapons as well as a hierarchy of suggested drilling concepts. I feel certain that drilling these concepts with diligence will take your game to the next level and beyond. Good luck and good training.

Shadow boxing

Resources

Here are a few resources that you might find useful to augment your training.

My first recommendation is to please visit my Web site at **www.extremeselfprotection.com**. There you will find even more training material as well as updates and further resources. Also, please feel free to contact me with any questions, comments or concerns about the material presented.

Paladin Press
www.paladin-press.com
Paladin carries many training resources. They carry some of my videos/DVDs including the Extreme Boxing series that augments this material nicely. They also publish two superior texts on Muay Thai:

Muay Thai Kickboxing by Chad Boykin

Fighting Strategies of Muay Thai by Mark Van Schuyver

Ringside Boxing
www.ringside.com
Best choice for primo equipment.

Threat Response Solutions
www.trsdirect.com
The marketing is shrill but they carry my *Illegal Boxing* title that may be useful for visual demonstrations of some of the material found in this book. They also have the Grounded series for the "man caught on the mat with a standing opponent dilemma."

Tracks Publishing
www.startupsports.com

Yep, this very book's publisher. Tracks published our first two books on the grappling aspects of the NHB game ...

No Holds Barred Fighting by Mark Hatmaker

More No Holds Barred Fighting: Killer Submissions by Mark Hatmaker

... and three fine boxing texts:

Boxer's Start-Up by Doug Werner and Alan Lachica
Fighting Fit by Doug Werner and Alan Lachica
Boxing Mastery by Mark Hatmaker

Index